HER MAJESTY'S AMERICAN

BAEN BOOKS by STEVE WHITE

HER MAJESTY'S AMERICAN

STEVE WHITE

A Baen Books Original

Baen Publishing Enterprises
P.O. Box 1403
Riverdale, NY 10471
www.baen.com

ISBN: 978-1-4814-8342-1

Cover art by Dominic Harman

First printing, September 2018

Distributed by Simon & Schuster
1230 Avenue of the Americas
New York, NY 10020

Library of Congress Cataloging-in-Publication Data

Names: White, Steve, 1946– author.
Title: Her Majesty's American / Steve White.
Description: Riverdale, NY : Baen, [2018]
Identifiers: LCCN 2018023359 | ISBN 9781481483421 (trade pb)
Subjects: LCSH: Space warfare—Fiction. | BISAC: FICTION / Science Fiction / Space Opera. | FICTION / Science Fiction / Adventure. | FICTION / Science Fiction / Military. | FICTION / Alternative History.
Classification: LCC PS3573.H474777 H47 2018 | DDC 813/.54—dc23
LC record available at https://lccn.loc.gov/2018023359

10 9 8 7 6 5 4 3 2 1

Pages by Joy Freeman (www.pagesbyjoy.com)
Printed in the United States of America

TIMELINE OF THE BRITANNIC FEDERAL EMPIRE

(Events common to this timeline and ours in italics)

1688 – *The Glorious Revolution. William of Orange becomes King William III of England.*

1689 – William III and Queen Mary unexpectedly produce a male heir.

1690 – English Act of Settlement amended to exclude Anne, the daughter of James II. Descendants of William and Mary confirmed as English monarchs as well as Princes of Orange (with all that implied regarding the Dutch stadholdership).

1702–1713 – First *War of the Spanish Succession*. Hanover joins on Anglo-Dutch side due to collateral dynastic connection. Existing tacit agreement that India is an English sphere of influence and the East Indies a Dutch one is formalized, and the Dutch are confirmed in perpetual possession of the Cape Colony, subject to certain English naval concessions.

1702 – *Death of William III of England.* His thirteen-year-old son Maurice crowned king, at first with a regency council. As Prince of Orange, he also becomes Stadholder of Holland and other Dutch provinces.

1707 – *Act of Union, creating kingdom of Great Britain.* King Maurice I comes of age.

1713 – First *War of the Spanish Succession ends. Spanish Bourbons excluded from French succession.*

1740–1748 – *War of the Austrian Succession.* Austrian Netherlands partitioned between France and the United Netherlands.

1756–1763 – *Seven Years' War; at its end, Britain has Canada, Florida and a dominant position in India.* France keeps Louisiana.

1775 – First *American Rebellion begins.*

1778 – Rapprochement reached between North American rebels and British Crown, with strong support of King William V and George Washington, the erstwhile rebel military commander

Extremists among the rebels, concentrated in New England and led by General Benedict Arnold, refuse to accept the agreement. Over the next two years, British and American Loyalist forces led by Washington suppress them.

1780 – Fighting in North America ends. Arnold and other rebel leaders hanged. Irreconcilable ex-rebel emigrants depart for French Louisiana and Spanish Texas, in both of which they eventually become the dominant element.

1781 – Settlement of North American issues finalized. Colonies reorganized into smaller number of dominions, within Vice-royalty of North America (although Canada remains classified as a province); Imperial Grand Council instituted.

1789 – *French Estates General*; the Comte de Mirabeau masterminds a British-style settlement.

1811 – British finalize treaty with loose confederation of Algonquin tribes under Tecumseh; Dominion of Indiana formed.

1830 – Indian uprising in northern Louisiana; St. Louis destroyed.

1851 – The Bourbon king of Spain dies without issue. In the absence of any apparent heir, the French (who have never given up their dream of uniting the two monarchies) put forward the current heir to the French throne as the nearest relation.

1852 – Second American Rebellion begins; Robert E. Lee rises rapidly in the rebel command after a series of victories.

1853–1856 – Second War of the Spanish Succession. Prussia, Russia and Britain intervene to prevent Franco-Spanish union. Austria and Hanover (whose Anglo-Dutch dynastic link has lapsed) side with France.

1854 – Viewing the American uprising as a distraction from events in Europe, Britain agrees to further reforms, including the finalization of the Imperial Grand Council's development into a super-legislature, in which the dominions are directly represented;

the Viceroyalty of North America continues to exist within the Imperial structure, dealing with specific interdominion North American matters. These reforms put an end to the rebellion except for the still-intransigent Dominion of New England, where an independent commonwealth is declared with tacit Britain consent, putting an effective end to the fighting.

1855 – French governor of Louisiana realizes that France is losing the war. With the support of the descendants of the American rebels who moved there, he declares an independent kingdom, securing his position by an alliance of convenience with the British, who take the northern parts (and the Indian problem).

1856 – Peace of Vienna; Spanish throne goes to a very distant Bourbon relation; France forced to recognize independence of Kingdom of Louisiana; British officially recognize independence of Commonwealth of New England.

1857–1858 – *Great Mutiny leads to winding up of British East India Company* and foundation of Viceroyalty of India; King William VII adds "Emperor of India" and "Emperor of North America" to his titles, although the term "empire" has already been used for almost a century.

1861–1862 – Scattered revolts in North America, put down by the Viceroyalty's forces, led by Lee; these prove to have been instigated by the Commonwealth of New England, and covertly aided by Louisiana and American émigrés in Texas.

1863 – British North America, provoked, reconquers Commonwealth of New England.

1865 – British North America conquers Louisiana.

1867 – Ex-commonwealth and Louisianan adventurers and mercenaries who have drifted into Texas combine with the ex-rebel element already established there to aid, and then take control of, a revolutionary movement against the Spanish monarchy; Viceroyalty of New Spain is declared the United States of Mexico.

1868 – Dominion of Canada created within Viceroyalty of North America; Hudson Bay Company compensated for loss of some holdings with large land grants in Great Plains.

1870 – After a revolt in Red River area, Hudson Bay Company nationalized and Dominion of Manitoba created.

1876 – Gold discovered in Russian America; Russian colonization increases.

1881 – British and Spanish empires combine to overthrow the United States of Mexico; Britain takes Texas, which eventually attains dominion status over the following decade; the Sioux transfer allegiance from the Spanish to the British Crown.

1882 – Russian annexation of Manchuria; Manchu China descends into warlordism.

1883 – Term "Imperial Federation" first used.

1893–1896 – Succession struggle in Russia. The brother of the (deceased) loser flees to Russian America and declares it an independent grand duchy.

1885 – Ireland granted dominion status, with its own parliament.

1898 – Spanish government reformed; attempts to integrate Spanish America with Spain along the lines of British Imperial Federation begin.

1901 – British provinces in Australia united as a dominion.

1907 – New Zealand granted dominion status.

1907–1912 – First Near Eastern War between Russia and Triple Alliance of Austria, France and Prussia, stemming from Russian intervention in Turkey. In the end, a peace of exhaustion brokered by Britain dismembers Turkey into spheres of influence.

1945 – Viceroyalty of India (heretofore an anomaly in the theory of Imperial Federation) granted representation in the Imperial Grand Council even though it is not composed of self-governing dominions.

1958–1970 – Second Near Eastern War, originally between Triple Alliance and Russia. Initially limited to the Near East as before, the fighting eventually spreads to Europe. British Empire remains neutral.

1959 – One warlord finally unites China.

1968 – British Empire joins the war on the side of the Triple Alliance and begins to secretly develop nuclear weapons.

1970 – War ends when British Empire threatens to use nuclear weapons. Russia collapses in revolution. Prussia annexes Poland.

Otherwise, the allies leave the struggling new Republic of Russia alone. British fleet shields the Grand Duchy of Alaska. Islamic Caliphate arises out of the ruins of the Turkish Empire, but at first is regarded as ignorable by Western powers as it is willing to do business with respect to petroleum.

1972 – Dictatorship seizes power in Russia, puts down a rebellion in Manchuria (China is still too weak to prevent this).

1977 – Quintuple Alliance formed (Spain and British Empire joining the old Triple Alliance) against Russia.

1992 – British attempt to normalize relations with Russia; one result is that Russia steals secret of nuclear weapons.

2002–2005 – Russian War, fought with conventional weapons under a nuclear standoff.

2005 – War ends as coup topples Russian regime when dictator orders all-out nuclear strike. Chinese take advantage of the situation to seize Russian-held Korea and Manchuria. Russian monarchy reconstituted under grand-ducal house of Alaska.

2008 – Principle of Imperial Federation extended to Britain itself; England and Scotland become dominions, on same footing as others. This removes the last vestige of the dichotomy between metropolis and colonies. The name Britannic Federal Empire becomes official.

2021–2028 – Muslim jihad against Western influence in Near East. Islamic Caliphate expands and is taken over by extreme fundamentalists.

2043 – Greater China declared.

2120 – Colonizing expedition of North American separatists departs for fifty-five-year voyage to Tau Ceti.

2170 – Bernheim Drive invented.

2175 – North American separatists arrive at Tau Ceti to find Imperial outpost already established there by an expedition which traveled from Earth under Bernheim Drive in nine and a half days. They are nonetheless allowed to found their colony on the planet New America.

2281 – The present.

"I never had an idea of subduing the Americans;
I meant to assist the good Americans to subdue the bad."
—*General James Robertson*

"England has left Europe altogether behind it
and has become a world state."
—*John Robert Seeley*

"I would annex the planets if I could."
—*Cecil Rhodes*

HER MAJESTY'S AMERICAN

CHAPTER ONE

IT WAS APRIL, BUT THIS WAS LONDON.

Ever since his return several days earlier, Commander Robert Rogers, RSN, had endured chill drizzle and told himself not to think longingly of what the weather was probably like just now in his native Dominion of Virginia. He had also reflected, not for the first time, that it was easy to understand how the Empire had come to be. Small wonder that so many people in earlier centuries had been so willing, if not eager, to leave England.

Today, however, had come a break in the weather. The overcast had thinned sufficiently for the sun to shine through in a pallid sort of way, and a fine mist rose from the still-damp streets of the old city where they were struck by that hazy radiance. So Rogers felt in a more positive frame of mind as he left his lodgings just off the King's Road and got into his glide car. In fact, as the glide car proceeded through Chelsea on its fixed-altitude grav repulsion (full-capability aircars were, of course, not allowed over central London), he permitted himself the luxury of appreciating the fact that the most direct route to his office through the labyrinth of streets was also a scenic route.

Indeed, although he did not often admit it, he was far from immune to the ambience of antiquity that clung to this old city that was still the capital of the Britannic Federal Empire, not

1

just because of its historic primacy but because it was a good compromise between today's power centers of North America and India. The gleaming towers of twenty-third century Greater London could be glimpsed through the mist in the distance, but here a sedate reverence for tradition reigned. As he turned left onto Grosvenor Place, he could look to the right and see the rear elevation of what was still called Buckingham House, although the townhouse of the Dukes of Buckingham had, beginning after 1781, been acquired by the monarchy and subsequently remodeled and enlarged repeatedly as the meeting place of the Imperial Grand Council. Presently Hyde Park was on his left, with the Serpentine and Kensington Gardens beyond and, invisible from here despite its monumental size, Kensington Palace, the principal residence of the Queen-Empress. Proceeding north through Mayfair and St. Marylebone, he soon passed to the right of Nassau Park, which had never entirely lost its semi-rustic character and was fringed with villas in the style known as Third Neo-Renaissance. Then he entered a region where the architecture rapidly shaded over into modernity even though the height restrictions were still applicable. This was the home of a number of governmental agencies of non-traditional character, most notably the particularly large and distinctly modern one which was his destination: the headquarters of the Royal Space Navy.

Sliding into the subterranean car park, he alighted and rode the lift to the central lobby, a large hexagonal space, its walls decorated with holographs of illustrious space warships of various generations. It was already thronged by personnel, most of them in RSN black, white and silver, some in the scarlet, black and gold of the Royal Marines. This uniformity of dress was not reflected in the people who wore them, for the RSN was an integrated Empire-wide service. There were numerous representatives of the Viceroyalty of India's various ethnicities, African-descended subjects of various origins, and the occasional subject from this or that extrasolar dominion whose face and form had been molded by extreme environment and sometimes by genetic engineering into something not quite like any familiar Earthly type.

In fact, not even the dress was altogether uniform, for a fair number of people were in civilian suits—not just civilian employees, but also officers who customarily reported to duty so attired. Rogers was one. He went to the central desk and casually submitted his identification to the duty officer, who knew him well, and then walked over to a particular lift with special security warnings and even more special sensors. He paused and submitted to scanning by those sensors, which confirmed his DNA profile and permitted the door to iris open. He entered the "up" tube and let the tractor beam effect take him. He ascended to a level accessible only to this lift and a couple of others like it, and stepped out into a relatively uncrowded, almost hushed precinct inhabited mostly by people in civilian dress, moving about with purposeful intent. There was little ornamentation here, and nothing to indicate to the uninitiated that this was the nerve center of Naval Intelligence.

Proceeding along a corridor toward his office, he chided himself for the ennui that was steadily eclipsing his earlier good mood. It had been only a few days since he had returned from his last assignment to the Zeta Tucanae system and the leave of absence which had followed it, and he had no business being already bored with paperwork. At this rate, how long could he expect to last?

Besides, after some of his experiences at Zeta Tucanae, there was something to be said for boredom.

He hadn't quite reached his office when the tiny short-range communicator implanted in his skull dinged for attention. He made the motion with his jaw that activated it. "Yes?" he acknowledged, subvocalizing out of habit.

"The director wants you, Bob." The speaker didn't need to identify himself, for the voice in Rogers' head was the familiar one of Commander Gopal Singh, the chief of staff.

"On my way." Rogers turned on his heel and retraced his steps to the Intelligence floor's central hub. There he made a ninety-degree turn into another corridor. As he walked along a certain segment, he knew that he was being examined by another passive DNA scanner, and that if he hadn't passed muster his every voluntary muscle would have been instantly paralyzed. It was easy to understand why there was no guard at the corridor's final door: no unauthorized person got as far as the director's office. Still, there was one final scan before the door opened and Rogers entered the waiting room. It had two occupants. One was the director's secretary/receptionist—human, a major status symbol in itself, and in fact a very sightly if somewhat severe female one at that. The other was a sturdily built blond man in civilian clothes who rose to his feet with a smile and extended his hand.

"Hello, Bob," he said in the only slightly accented English spoken nowadays by practically all citizens of the Dutch Republic. "It's been a while."

"Too long a while, Adrian," said Rogers, taking the proffered hand and trying to conceal his surprise at seeing a non-Imperial subject here. But, on reflection, he decided it wasn't all that startling. Adrian de Graeff was a well-respected professional colleague who had worked with Naval Intelligence before. And besides, being Dutch wasn't *quite* the same thing as being foreign. After all, in addition to be being Queen of England, Scotland and Ireland (the old claim to the throne of France had, somewhere along the line, been quietly dropped), Empress of North America, Empress of India, et cetera, Mary II was also Princess of Orange and therefore *ex officio* Stadholder of Holland, Zealand, Utrecht and Gelderland.

It was a state of affairs that, like so much else, had its origin in the fact that shortly after the Glorious Revolution of 1688 William of Orange, newly become King William III of England, and his wife Mary had, to the general astonishment of all (especially considering the unsubstantiated but persistent rumors about William's proclivities) produced a male heir. That heir, after appropriate adjustments to the Act of Settlement, had inherited the English Crown, thus preventing it from going to James II's childless daughter Anne, which could have had all sorts of unpredictable dynastic effects—possibly even casting the crown to George, Elector of Hanover, as the nearest (however remote) Protestant heir. He had also inherited the Principality of Orange, and his heirs had continued to do so from that day to this, since all concerned had long since amended their succession laws in favor of the first-born heir regardless of gender. Something else that had continued unbroken was the custom of the four principal states of the Netherlands automatically appointing the incumbent Prince of Orange to the stadholdership. (The other states, just to be different, appointed their stadholders from a cadet branch of the House of Orange.) Thus it was that the monarch of the Britannic Federal Empire was also the ceremonial head of the Dutch Republic—and, in theory, the commander in chief of its armed forces, for the Prince of Orange also automatically became Captain General and Admiral General of the United Provinces.

It was an anomalous situation that peoples concerned with logic and systemization—the French, for example—would never have lived with. But it seemed to suit the English and Dutch speakers. And it had provided every coalition against a would-be hegemonic European power—France, for example—with an unbreakable Anglo-Dutch backbone. That backbone had fortunately grown to dinosaurian proportions by the time Russia had replaced France as the power threatening to bestride the continent, as Britain's overseas empire had grown and knitted together in accordance with the great principle of Imperial Federation. And the special— indeed, unique—relationship had endured to the present day.

Still, Rogers couldn't help wondering what had been important enough to warrant downloading De Graeff's DNA profile into the security system.

"What brings you here?" he asked. "Last I heard, you were working in Batavia." The Dutch Republic had never managed to integrate the East Indies into a federal imperial structure as successfully as the British had integrated India. Rogers rather complacently told himself that it probably had something to do with Dutch stubbornness. After all these centuries, they hadn't even yielded to persistent demands to change the name of Batavia to "Jakarta."

"I was—and that's what brings me here." The smile vanished. "I turned up something a little beyond our scope. The Council decided your lot needed to be involved."

Rogers nodded. The Dutch *Raad Terrorismebestrijding en Veiligheid* (Council for Counterterrorism and Security) routinely worked hand in glove with the various Imperial intelligence and security agencies, which, in the immemorial way of such things, had proliferated and overlapped over the centuries like jungle growth. But one thing in the bureaucratic thicket was fairly straightforward: Naval Intelligence had jurisdiction of matters beyond low Earth orbit, with the various security agencies of the extrasolar dominions subordinate to it wherever it chose to exercise that jurisdiction.

"So," he said, "you happened onto something with extraterrestrial connections. You must have been nosing around Singapura." A century earlier, after the invention of the Bernheim Drive, the most challenging part of interstellar flight had been the first eighty-four hundred miles, the distance from Earth's surface to the "Primary

Limit" where the drive could be activated. The obvious solution had been a space elevator, providing cheap transportation to a space terminal at a geostationary point well outside the Primary Limit. An Anglo-Dutch corporation had been chartered for the purpose, and the Dutch had offered as the Earthside terminus the island of Singapura at the southern tip of the Malay Peninsula, almost exactly on the equator. Then the advent of grav repulsion had rendered the whole concept obsolete. But by that time a great deal of infrastructure had been put in place on Singapura, which the canny Dutch weren't about to let go to waste. Today the island was one of Earth's principal spaceports... and a very cosmopolitan place, with all the security headaches that implied.

"Yes I was." De Graeff frowned. "But I probably ought to wait to tell you the details, until—"

A bell tone sounded on the receptionist's desk, and she looked up with an institutional expression. "Commander Rogers, Mynheer De Graeff, the director will see you now."

The two men passed through an old-fashioned door into a spacious office decorated in the elegant style known as Mauricean since it dated to the reign of Maurice II in the early nineteenth century. Oil paintings of various long-deceased luminaries (and, of course, Her Majesty) hung on the walls, and shelves were lined with old-fashioned books. The furnishings were in the same style, and the large desk was particularly fine, but it incorporated an array of modern equipment, including a computer with the capability of projecting a holographic display, and a communicator link with the powerful lasercom on the building's roof, linked in turn to the interplanetary-range installation in orbit.

The elderly man behind the desk motioned them toward chairs, peering out from under crusty gray eyebrows.

"Have a seat, gentlemen." Vice Admiral Sir Angus Fraser, Director of Naval Intelligence, was from the Dominion of Canada, but his accent seemed to owe more to his Scottish parents. "Mynheer De Graeff, I'm obliged for your prompt arrival. I'll let you explain to Commander Rogers here the reason we requested your presence. Don't bother with the details—you'll be able to brief him on those after he's read your full report." He busied himself with loading his trademark pipe with genetically engineered noncarcinogenic tobacco.

"Of course, Admiral." De Graeff turned to Rogers. "As you

surmised, Bob, I've been in Singapura. We had gotten indications that the Caliphate has been trying an indirect approach to infiltration, through one of their extrasolar colonies."

Rogers nodded. The Islamic Caliphate's attempts to stir up disaffection among the Muslim populations of the Viceroyalty of India and also of the Dutch East Indies were a fact of international life (so far on the level of a chronic, low-grade, publicly unacknowledged irritant, inasmuch as the Caliphate's grimly fundamentalist version of Islam had made little headway among those populations). And over the past generation the Caliphate had managed to rationalize away its own technophobic ideology to the point of planting some colonies among the stars—sometimes bringing it into confrontation with the Empire.

"As you undoubtedly know," De Graeff explained, "the Caliphate colony in the Psi Capricorni system has begun exporting a significant amount of rare elements, and quite a lot of this traffic comes through Singapura. We've gotten indications that they're trying to use this as a conduit for infiltration, bypassing our usual security measures around the East Indies. Recently, we've managed to apprehend a couple of their lower-level operatives—actually more useful to us for interrogation purposes, since the higher-ups almost always have ingenious suicide devices."

"I know," said Rogers. "The other side of the coin is that the low-rankers simply don't know very much."

"True. But we were able to get a few useful leads about Caliphate activities." De Graeff paused significantly. "One of which points in the direction of New America."

"*What?*" Rogers couldn't keep the surprised bewilderment out of his voice. "But what possible connection could there be?"

"That's precisely what we want to find out," said Sir Angus, who by now had puffed his pipe to aromatic life. "And now you know why you're here, Commander. I'm sending you to the Tau Ceti system where you'll investigate this matter in conjunction with the local authorities on New America."

"Er . . . that could be a bit awkward, sir. Given New America's unique and rather ill-defined relationship to the Empire, it won't be just a matter—"

"Of you walking in and ordering the locals about," Sir Angus finished for him. "It will call for a bit more diplomacy than that. Which is why I've chosen you. Among those who are North

Americans, you're the best-qualified officer currently available. A common background should be of assistance in working smoothly with the famously touchy colonials there."

Rogers grew expressionless and spoke carefully. "I should point out, sir, that I may not be the most tactful choice for dealing with the New Americans. Given my family history...my very name, in fact—"

"Yes, yes, I know," Sir Angus cut in with a touch of impatience. "But as I say, all my other North American senior investigating agents are otherwise occupied at the moment, or simply aren't up to you in terms of qualifications. And after all," he added in a more soothing tone, "that's all ancient history, isn't it? It's been five hundred years since the First North American Rebellion, and over a century since New America was colonized. I'll wager the New Americans you'll be working with won't even know who the original Robert Rogers was."

Out of the corner of his eye, Rogers saw De Graeff's puzzlement.

"Perhaps not, sir. But I understand those people have very long memories."

CHAPTER TWO

"WHAT ON EARTH WERE YOU AND THE OLD MAN TALKING ABOUT?" asked Adrian de Graeff. "It was all beyond me."

"Yes, I could tell you were a bit mystified there, at the end." Rogers studied his wine glass moodily, gazing through the prism of his white bordeaux at the officers' canteen where the two of them were having lunch. "Well, the fact of the matter is, I'm a direct descendant of—and, in fact, named after—one of New America's historical villains."

"I *knew* it!" De Graeff slapped his knee delightedly. "I've always suspected there was something sinister about you. What you need are black mustachios suitable for twirling."

"No joke," said Rogers with a wan smile. "Oh, not one of their *major* villains, you understand. Like George Washington, who accepted the rapprochement that ended the First American Rebellion and then went on to lead the loyalist forces against Benedict Arnold's die-hard rebels. Or Robert E. Lee, who played a similar role about eighty years later; he had been one of the rising stars of the Second Rebellion, but he was reconciled to the concessions that the British Crown made to end the Rebellion, and later he put down the uprisings instigated by the breakaway Commonwealth of New England, which he subsequently reconquered."

9

"Er...I'm afraid North American history isn't exactly my subject."

"Then you almost certainly won't have heard of the original Robert Rogers. He was a hero of the French and Indian War—the Seven Years' War to you. His instructions for his outfit, Rogers' Rangers, are still considered a model for special forces. But after that war, he was a disaster as a frontier administrator...and, it seems, a bit of a crook. In fact, he ended up in debtors' prison in England. Then, after the First Rebellion broke out, he returned to America, where he was arrested as a British spy by Washington, who at that time was still leading the rebels. He escaped, and formed a new unit of loyalist rangers. After the peace settlement, when they found themselves on the same side, he was reconciled with Washington, and seems to have recovered his old flair. He was instrumental in putting down Arnold's rebel holdouts. In the end, he led one of his trademark daring raids and captured Arnold, who was subsequently hanged—and who is now regarded on New America as a martyr."

A low whistle escaped De Graeff. "I can see how the New Americans might not exactly remember your eponymous ancestor with fond affection."

"Scarcely." Rogers chuckled. "You can probably also understand why the family found it advisable to leave its original homeland of New England—always the hotbed of rebel sentiment, you know—and move to the Dominion of Virginia, where we've been ever since."

De Graeff's brow furrowed, and he spoke with the almost impeccable Briticism he had picked up over the years. "But I say, old man, I'm confused. I've always been under the impression that Washington and Lee are remembered as heroes in North America."

"Indeed they are. In fact, they've been so regarded by most North Americans for almost three centuries, and by practically all North Americans nowadays, when we and India are the twin pillars of the Federal Empire. But we're not talking about modern North Americans. We're talking about *New* Americans."

"Ah, yes—those colonials. I confess I've never been entirely clear on where they stand vis-à-vis the Empire. I know, of course, that they are the descendants of humanity's first, last and only attempt at slower-than-light interstellar colonization."

"Right. You see, as late as the early twenty-second century there were still some irreconcilable separatists in North America. After a habitable planet was detected at Tau Ceti, they formed an organization called 'New America,' dedicated to establishing a colony so far away that it would *have* to be independent. The Empire was very accommodating about letting them try."

"Must have been barely possible—and bloody expensive—with the technology they had then."

"Yes: antimatter pion rocket, and magnetic sail for deceleration and in-system maneuvering once they arrived. But the Empire was generous with financial help. Of course you, having a nasty, cynical turn of mind, are doubtless thinking this generosity might have had something to do with wanting to get rid of some troublesome malcontents."

"I'd *never* suggest such a thing!" De Graeff was the picture of wronged innocence.

"Anyway," Rogers continued, ignoring him, "they departed in 2120 for Tau Ceti. It was a fifty-five-year voyage, which they spent in cryogenic suspension. But while they were still in flight, with only a few years to go, Bernheim invented the warp drive back on Earth. An expedition using his drive went to Tau Ceti in nine and a half days and founded an outpost there. So when the New Americans arrived and came out of suspended animation—"

"The first thing they saw was the Union Jack," De Graeff finished for him. "What a miserably rotten disappointment!"

"I understand they considered it a bit of a letdown," said Rogers dryly. It occurred to him that he had been in England too long; he was picking up the habit of studied understatement. "Still, the Empire was quite decent about it, and didn't stand on its rights as the first to land and establish occupancy. The New Americans were permitted to go ahead and plant their colony, and even name the planet 'New America.' Since then, they've enjoyed a sort of ill-defined self-governing status."

"Yes—that's the part I've never quite grasped, as I mentioned before."

"They're quite self-governing internally. Of course, there's an Imperial resident commissioner to sort of oversee things."

"Of course," De Graeff echoed, deadpan.

"Well, for one thing, there was the matter of the franchise," said Rogers, just a trifle defensively. "There is, after all, a minority descended from the Imperial settlers—who, at least arguably, have a better right to be there than the New Americans. A certain degree of Imperial supervision has been necessary to prevent discrimination against them. It's a case of history repeating itself; the Puritan oligarchy of seventeenth- and eighteenth-century New England could never resist the temptation to weigh the scales in favor of the godly, unless restrained from doing so by the Crown. I believe," he added parenthetically, with a tight smile, "that they considered my own Scotch-Irish ancestors distinctly ungodly." He tossed off most of his wine, dismissing the subject. "Anyway, they have a standing offer of dominion status, with full representation on the Imperial Grand Council. They've never accepted it."

"Fancy that!" De Graeff's irony was arch.

Rogers shot him a glance. "Hmm...I suppose it's really not too surprising, is it? Still, it would simplify things if they did. More to the point, it would make my job easier if I didn't have to deal with a lot of autonomous local security and law-enforcement people."

"The courier service will let them know you're coming, and why. Hopefully, they'll assign you a liaison officer who takes a cooperative attitude. And surely they can't like the Caliphate any more than we do."

"They may not like it, but at the same time they may not take it very seriously as a threat. Remember, while there's undoubtedly the odd Indian-descended Muslim among the Imperial people there, there are none among the New Americans themselves. So I wouldn't put it past them to brush it off as our problem, not theirs."

"Still, they can't ignore the evidence I turned up."

"You may underestimate their capacity for parochialism," said Rogers dourly. He finished off his wine. "However, let's go and review that evidence. I'll read through your report and then later we can go over it in detail. From what I've heard so far, I'll need some more convincing."

It was six o'clock when Rogers spoke an irritable command, and the computer's holographic display above the desk vanished. He sat back, stretched, and bestowed a disappointed look on De Graeff.

"This is pretty thin stuff, Adrian."

"Well," the Dutchman protested, "admittedly the individuals we caught had no direct link to any operation on New America. But the fact remains that one of them, under questioning with drugs and so forth, revealed knowledge of others who had such links."

"But he had no idea what, specifically, those others were up to."

"Remember, these were low-level members of a highly compartmentalized organization. We're lucky they knew even as much as they did."

"But what can it possibly mean? What can the connection be? As tiresome as the New Americans can sometimes be, I'm the first to admit that their values and ideals are poles apart from those of the bloody Caliphate."

"Still," De Graeff reminded him, deploying the final, unanswerable argument, "It's sufficient to arouse the Old Man's interest. And his wishes are our command."

"True," Rogers sighed. He glanced at the time. "Well, to hell with it for now. I told you I'd take you to dinner. There's a place I go to often that will make you understand why I've finally acquired a taste for English cooking."

"I look forward to having my skepticism dispelled," said De Graeff rather heavily.

They threaded their way through ancient London. The feeling of an old, dark, mysterious city grew even more pronounced as the narrow, crooked streets became permeated with mist—seemingly the mists of antiquity. But the mood had evaporated by the time they arrived at the not-too-conspicuous entrance to Hobart's Restaurant on a side street just off the Strand.

"The grilled Scotch salmon here is one of London's well-kept secrets," Rogers assured De Graeff as they proceeded to their table. "And they've been in this location forever."

"It looks it," said De Graeff, gazing around at the heavy oaken timbers crossing the plaster ceiling, and the dark oak-paneled bar.

Rogers was thinking the same thing. This, he told himself, was the concentrated and distilled essence of Old London, with its reassuring atmosphere of tradition, stability and order...

All at once, like an alarm disrupting a deep dream, a discordant note entered into his consciousness—a subliminal psychic tingling that had always signaled danger, and had never been mistaken.

At a table just ahead of them and to the right, a man was sitting with his back to them. Somehow, a split second before it happened, Rogers knew that man was going to stand up and turn around to face them. It probably saved his life, for he was already starting to twist aside when the man reached inside his jacket and whipped out a weapon—*Svoboda-Hoche Model 2279 needler* flashed through Rogers' brain automatically—and swung it from side to side. There was a sharp crackling as a stream of electromagnetically accelerated steel flechettes broke the sound barrier in the restaurant's confined spaces.

But Rogers was already ducking under that fusillade and launching himself forward. With the restaurant still suspended in a state of shock, he crashed into the man and wrestled him to the floor, one hand grasping the Svoboda-Hoche and sending its spray of needlelike projectiles cracking into the plaster of the ceiling, and the other arm going around the man's throat. It brought their faces close together—close enough for Rogers to smell the man's breath and take in a fleeting impression of his olive-complexioned face. Then the man's jaws clamped shut as he bit down at a certain angle, and Rogers heard a *snap* whose import he recognized. Instantly, he released his opponent and rolled away, turning his back and pulling a chair over behind him. That chair probably saved him, for it was barely down when a small but sharp explosion rang out. He, along with everyone else nearby, was showered with blood, brains and bone slivers.

The spell of shock was broken, and the restaurant erupted into screaming panic. Ignoring that pandemonium, Rogers turned over to face the shooter's headless body. Its neck was a ragged stump from which blood was still weakly pumping. He sat up, and saw that De Graeff was down.

He scrambled to the Dutchman's side, shouting, "Somebody send for a doctor!" But his shout went unheard in the stampede, as everyone able to move frantically crowded out of the restaurant with its stench of death. And he saw that it was too late anyway. One of the things—besides its small size and concealability—that made the Svoboda-Hoche a favorite assassin's weapon was that its long needles were unstable in flesh. They disintegrated against body armor, but they did vicious internal damage to an unarmored target. Blood was already oozing from De Graeff's mouth.

"Stay with me, Adrian!" he pleaded. But by the time the last of the fleeing restaurant patrons had struggled out into the street he was alone with a few moaning, injured bystanders and two corpses.

✧　　✧　　✧

"The police have naturally run a DNA scan on the shooter's body," Gopal Singh reported. "But it doesn't match anyone they have on file. All it proves is that he was almost certainly of Near Eastern ancestry. Of course they're pursuing all other avenues, and we're extending them every possible assistance."

"Of course," said Sir Angus morosely.

"I think it's safe to say," the chief of staff went on, "that Commander Rogers was the target. After all, he's a regular patron of that restaurant."

"Still, the matter on which he was working with De Graeff may be related to the motivation for the attack. In other words, it may not be just a coincidence that this happened at this particular time. I want you to investigate the possibility that there could be a leak within this office, by which they would have known that the two of them were going to dinner together." Sir Angus turned to hitherto-silent Rogers and, uncharacteristically, addressed him by his first name. "I'm sorry, Robert. I know he was a friend as well as a professional colleague."

"Thank you, sir," Rogers said mechanically. With most of his consciousness, he was assuring himself over and over that Adrian's death was not his fault. *Who knows?* he thought. *Eventually, I may even succeed in convincing myself.*

"We may wish to delay your departure for Tau Ceti," the director went on, "pending further investigation of this...incident. And also giving you a chance to—"

"That's quite all right, sir. Please don't delay anything on my account. In fact, I'd like to depart as soon as possible. You see, I now take Adrian's investigation with great seriousness. And besides...it's become personal."

CHAPTER THREE

SIR ANGUS HAD, FROM THE FIRST, WANTED ROGERS' ARRIVAL ON New America to be inconspicuous. What had happened at Hobart's had caused him to upgrade "inconspicuous" to "clandestine."

This suited Rogers for any number of reasons, not the least of which was that he would use civilian transportation instead of a fast but austere Navy courier craft. Of course, the Regal Lines' sleekly up-to-date passenger liner *Queen Elizabeth IV* wasn't precisely slow; she would cover the twelve light-years to Tau Ceti, her first port of call, in less than two and a half standard days. Some additional time was taken up by orbital transfers at each end; not even grav repulsion made it practical for a ship of *Queen Elizabeth IV*'s size to land on planets. Thus it was that Rogers rode a shuttle from Salisbury Plain Spaceport up to the great oblate spheroid that was Albion Space Station, where he went through the relatively painless red tape of routine clearance before being allowed to proceed through an access tube to the ship, where it was moored against one of the station's great docking flanges.

After depositing his minimal luggage in his stateroom, Rogers decided he had time for a before-dinner drink. The ship's lounge was a large hemispherical chamber, which was one great television receiver, so that it was like sitting on the outside of the hull surrounded on all sides but astern by the star-blazing firmament and the cloud-marbled curve of Earth slightly more than a thousand miles below, with the sun peeking over its edge. He had barely finished his scotch and soda and ordered another when the intercom announced imminent departure. Some of the inexperienced travelers who had been gawking at the panorama looked a trifle apprehensive at that, although they had been assured that there was no cause for alarm. Nor was there. All that happened was that the sternward blind zone was suddenly ringed with the fringes of the vast-spreading cone of light produced by the photon rockets, and Earth began to slide away and recede. The inertial compensators prevented anyone from feeling any sensation of acceleration, and they coordinated with the artificial gravity so smoothly that no one's drink was spilled. (There was a barely audible tinkling of glassware, and a few ripples on the surface of the scotch and soda. Rogers suspected that the captain would mention it to the chief engineer.)

Rogers hadn't quite finished dinner when another announcement filled the air of the lounge. Steady acceleration had brought *Elizabeth IV* to the Primary Limit: the distance from a large body (twelve and a half thousand miles from planetary center, in the case of Earth) where the force of gravity was less than 0.1 g. Here, the Bernheim Drive could be safely activated.

All at once, the glow of the photon torch was no longer seen and there was a very slight fluctuation of weight. With Earth now invisibly astern, there was no nearby reference point to give a visual sensation of rapidly increasing speed. But space was being folded in front of the ship, the folding process altering the properties of space to reduce normal gravity in that direction, and *Elizabeth IV* was now lunging outward at an acceleration of two hundred gees. A *pseudo*-acceleration, actually; the inertial compensators were no longer needed, for the ship's occupants would have been in a state of free fall had it not been for the artificial gravity generators.

Under that terrific but insensible impulse, it didn't take long to reach the "Secondary Limit," just short of the asteroid belt. Here, at a distance of somewhat more than two astronomical units, the Sun's gravity field was a negligible 0.0001 g. Now the Bernheim Drive could safely wrap negative energy—the so-called "warp field"—around the ship to change the shape of space and create a kind of bubble in space-time (referred to as "subspace") that could move faster than other parts of space-time, just as theory insisted the fabric of space had expanded far faster than c in the few microseconds when the universe was inflating after the Big Bang. Inside the bubble, space was not distorted and the ship was still traveling at sublight speeds, so no physical laws were violated. But the bubble itself was moving through space-time faster than light, so when the field was formed it instantly imparted what was in effect superluminal velocity. Just how fast that was depended on the number of massive drive coils and the amount of energy pumped into the drive. In the case of *Elizabeth IV*, it was slightly more than nineteen hundred times as fast as light. That wasn't nearly as fast as the upper limit—currently around 3,000 c—that could be obtained by drive coils accounting for a quarter of the ship's loaded mass. But the closer one approached that threshold, cumulative deformations in the drive field degraded its efficiency and lowered the marginal returns from more massive drive coils; and beyond it a point of diminishing returns was reached. So only vessels optimized for speed pushed the limit. A liner like *Elizabeth IV*, in no tearing hurry and intended to carry as many passengers as possible in the state of luxury they expected, followed the usual standard regarded as economically optimal for civilian ships: her drive coils accounted for ten percent of her total mass (about half of what was typical for naval combatants) with the other Bernheim Drive components (exclusive of powerplant) adding another four percent or so.

There was still no sense of movement when the ship's accumulators, charged by the inferno of energy that was its antimatter reactor, put out the tremendous surge of energy necessary to initially form the warp field. But this time there *was* a visual effect. It wasn't a necessary one. But the captain knew it was a thrill for the first-time passengers when he left the outside view unaltered at this moment. And as always, there was a chorus of gasps, and a scattering of squeals from the women, when the stars suddenly flowed swiftly sternward, flashing through the light-show of Doppler effects, before giving way to absolute void. But then the screens returned to reassuring steadiness, showing a virtual representation of the universe outside the field, as it would have looked in the (impossible) event that it could be seen normally from subspace. And even at the unthinkable pseudovelocity to which the ship had been instantly translated, the stars were too distant to show any visible motion.

Early in the second "day" of the voyage, Rogers activated his stateroom's computer and brought up the *Imperial Star Directory*, 34th edition, and consulted the entry for his destination.

TAU CETI

DISTANCE FROM SOL:	11.9 light-years
SPECTRAL TYPE:	G8v
MASS:	0.78 Sol
RADIUS:	0.793 Sol
LUMINOSITY:	0.55 Sol
TEMPERATURE:	...

Rogers scrolled rapidly down. He didn't need all this stuff...Ah!

PLANETARY SYSTEM

Number	Name	Mass (Earth=1.0)	Orbital Radius (AU)	Orbital Period (Earth days)
I	Hino	2.0	0.105	13.965
II	Oshagadea	3.1	0.195	35.362
III	Sesondowah	3.6	0.374	94.11
IV	Gunnodoyak	4.3	0.552	168.12
V(a)	Eithinoha	7.8	1.35	642.0
V(b)	New America	2.3	"	"

Rogers smiled at the names. The discoverers—by means of radial velocity planetary searches—had by then been running out of pantheons, and had used the deities of the Iroquois people of North America. Initially, when planet V had been regarded as a possible super-terrestrial abode of life, it had been given the name of Eithinoha, the Iroquois goddess of Earth. Later, when it had been found to be in fact a double planet, the secondary planet had been named "Onatha" after Eithinoha's daughter. Still later, the colonists had been allowed to rechristen it "New America," although some purists among the astronomers (especially at Oxford) still insisted on calling it "Onatha." As for the other planets, the New Americans had been perfectly happy to leave them with names of unimpeachable North American pedigree, unlike the Norse and Babylonian and

Egyptian and other outlandish god-names that had been plastered over other extrasolar planetary systems.

The *Directory* went on to describe the "debris disk" at a radius of 10 to 55 AU, containing so much dust that Tau Ceti could almost be said to have a "ring." It also contained ten times as much asteroidal rubble as that which orbited Sol, with all that implied for asteroid impacts on the planets. One of the asteroids, 13.5 AU from Tau Ceti and above the plane of the ecliptic, housed the Royal Space Navy's base in this system. It had been thought that such an unobtrusive location would be more tactful than one closer to New America. Of course, the base's name—Washington Station—was a shade less tactful, however appropriate it had undoubtedly seemed at the time.

Rogers clicked on the more interesting of the planets for details. Gunnodoyak orbited near the inner edge of the liquid-water zone, the Eithinoha/New America doublet just inside its outer edge. But Gunnodoyak's dense atmosphere had doomed it to a runaway greenhouse effect, leaving it a hell-like "super-Venus." Eithinoha was a "gas dwarf," or a "nebulous superterrestrial" planet as it was sometimes called: a superterrestrial with a thick, helium-rich atmosphere and a small, low-density core. But New America was a rocky "super-Earth" at the very lowest mass-figure for that classification, presumably captured by Eithinoha as a result of what was called a "binary-exchange reaction" in the remote past, much as Sol's Neptune had once captured Triton; a gas-planet moon so massive relative to its parent could not form in the normal course of things from a shared accretion disk. Had New America fallen on the same mass-over-density curve as the terrestrial planets of the Solar system, it would have had a surface gravity nearly half again that of Earth. But Tau Ceti was older than Sol, and had formed out of an interstellar medium less enriched by supernovas. Hence it, and therefore its planets, had a lesser allotment of heavy elements, and New America's density yielded a gravity of 1.19 g. That was still enough to hold a relatively dense atmosphere, and what had been a curse for Gunnodoyak had been a blessing for New America, which was reasonably comfortable in an orbital position where Earth would have been frigid except possibly for the tropics. It also helped that Eithinoha's tidal forces caused a certain flexing of New America's crust, resulting in friction that warmed the planet from within.

Tau Ceti, like all main sequence stars, was gradually growing brighter, and as a consequence its liquid-water zone had only recently (as astronomers, not to be confused with people, defined "recently") expanded outward to encompass the double planets' orbit. But New America had spent enough time in the extended life zone conferred by its atmosphere for life to have arisen and spread. That life took only primitive forms; in a system whose planets suffered asteroid strikes of "dinosaur killer" magnitude ten times as often as those of Sol, there had never been time for the kind of riotous speciation and long-term evolution that characterized Earth's biosphere. From the standpoint of colonization, this was a good thing all around: the atmosphere had a breathable percentage of oxygen, and imported Terran species expanded rapidly, pushing the native stuff out of the way. And, of course, there were no dangerous animals.

There were other plus factors as well. Even before interstellar flight, it had been theorized that "super-Earths" of tolerable gravity were the best bet for life-bearing—and therefore readily colonizable—worlds. A thicker atmosphere than Earth's implied more erosive weather, hence flatter topography, with shallow seas and island archipelagos, the ideal environment for life to arise and spread to the land. More importantly, such a planet would retain more internal heat, leading to a longer-lasting spinning molten core, generating a stronger protective magnetic field as well as longer-lasting volcanism and plate tectonics to regulate carbon cycling. New America had provided confirmation of all this. There was even a school of thought that held that a higher gravity than Earth's (within reason) was healthier for humans due to the increased exercise it enforced.

Rogers skimmed through the rest of the planet's physical parameters, and also the information on its history, population, government, et cetera. Most of this he already knew, at least in general terms, and he wanted to have as open a mind as possible when exposed to the viewpoint of the liaison officer he was going to be assigned—a certain Grey Goldson. The name was about all he knew, given the limitations of interstellar communication. Instantaneous communication via quantum entanglement was a theoretical possibility, but so far that was all it was, due to the staggering size and expense of the apparatus it would require. Messages between the stars had to be carried by ship, like messages between continents on Earth before the first undersea telegraph cables. And the courier services had a chronic backlog of message traffic, even though they were restricted to official Crown business and private users who were able and willing to pay whacking great fees.

A certain adaptability on his part, he decided, would bear cultivating.

Given Tau Ceti's lesser mass, its Secondary Limit was somewhat closer in than Sol's. At a cautious distance outside it, *Elizabeth IV*'s captain disengaged the drive field, lest the drive abruptly shut down and suffer a possibly very severe degree of physical damage as the warp field collapsed with a completeness exceeded only by that of his own career.

On the other hand, Eithinoha's Primary Limit, extending well beyond New America's, was considerably farther out than Earth's. So the Bernheim Drive drove the ship in sublight mode for a relatively short time, as the passengers crowded the lounge and watched the double-planet system approach. That approach grew more and more gradual as the ship decelerated, for its pseudovelocity must be brought down to zero before the drive was turned off altogether—as it had to be turned off before crossing that Primary Limit. Failure to do either would result in the same highly unfortunate consequences to ship and captain. Afterwards, the ship's intrinsic velocity was resumed. (It was, Rogers had often reflected, a very fortuitous characteristic of the drive, preventing fanatics from using it to make planet-killers of asteroids by accelerating them up to relativistic velocities. He wouldn't have put it past the Caliphate.)

Thus the passengers had plenty of time to watch Eithinoha—banded like larger gas-giant planets, but gray-green rather than the angry orange of its more massive, Jupiter-like kin—grow, with New America off to the side, showing the beautiful cloud-swirling blueness of a predominantly oceanic world. As the approach continued, New America appeared to swing around and partially occlude its larger companion.

Then, with the last of the pseudovelocity shedded just outside the Primary Limit, the Bernheim Drive stopped playing tricks with space. The ship shifted seamlessly to photon thrusters and proceeded toward the space terminal in low New America orbit.

CHAPTER FOUR

NEW AMERICA WAS TIDELOCKED TO EITHINOHA AS THEY REVOLVED around their common center of mass at a surprisingly narrow separation. The result was a "day" of 98.67 standard hours, with the enormous globe of Eithinoha eternally fixed in the sky, eclipsing Tau Ceti for the "inner" hemisphere that faced it during most of that hemisphere's daylight hours.

However, the planetary capital of New Philadelphia was in the "outer" hemisphere, though not far over the line. So Eithinoha was only partially visible from there, seemingly a low but supernaturally vast dome looming over the horizon. And the length of the day was actually convenient, being very close to a multiple of the twenty-four-hour rotation period to which the human race had spent its entire evolutionary history becoming accustomed. The New Americans still lived according to that twenty-four-hour pattern. They simply divided their planet's rotation into four "days," some of sunlight and some of night, each divided into twenty-four hours slightly longer than those of Earth. These days were fairly reliable in the outer hemisphere, where it was always night anyway when New America swung into Eithinoha's cone of darkness.

When Rogers landed, New America was still on the sunward side of Eithinoha but was swinging into the "night" portion of its long rotation. So as he stepped out of the passenger shuttle at New Philadelphia's Patrick Henry Spaceport, Tau Ceti—slightly smaller and a deeper yellow than Sol as seen from Earth—was near the end of its protracted sunset, even though it was morning by the planet's arbitrary clock. The following day would be all-dark. Although New Philadelphia, like most New American cities, was in the equatorial zone, the air was brisk. It was also somewhat denser than Earth's. Rogers had little difficulty adjusting to that, or to the higher gravity; as per standard procedure, *Elizabeth IV* had gradually increased its interior air pressure and artificial gravity in the course of the voyage until both simulated New American conditions. In two and a half standard days there had been little time for acclimatization, but Rogers was an old hand at such adjustments.

Behaving in character as a private citizen, Rogers hired a glide car and set out for New Philadelphia. The short drive, southward along the shore of the Columbian Ocean, gave him a chance to observe the scenery. To his right the low dome of Eithinoha rose above the ocean horizon, partially eclipsing the setting sun, seemingly too huge to be real, although viewed through the atmosphere it appeared almost ethereal, giving no hint of its massiveness. The ocean itself was effectively tideless; Eithinoha raised a permanent tidal bulge on the other hemisphere, which was why this one held most of the dry land. To Rogers' left, beyond the sandy bluffs overlooking the ocean, the land rose in the low hills characteristic of much of New America's terrain, a combined product of extensive tectonic activity and the smoothing-out erosion of a thick atmosphere. The vegetation was familiar, for in the course of a century Earth imports (sometimes genetically tweaked) had pretty much taken over—just as well, inasmuch as the local stuff, with its "right-handed" amino acids, had no proteins humans could use.

Presently the hills rose ahead, and New Philadelphia spread out at their foot, on an expanse of flat land that formed a harbor. It was a small city, its most notable structure being the capitol building that crowned one of the hills overlooking the generally low cityscape. But, as Rogers knew from his orientation, there were several hotels, of which the Travelers' Rest was considered the best. There, he found that accommodations were available. (Except for the most exalted of personages, there was no such thing as hotel reservations across interstellar distances. Certainly there were none for nondescript private citizens such as Rogers was supposed to be.) Once settled into his room, he called a certain number, using a wrist communicator with special security features.

"Patrick Logan here," said a voice holding the twang of the Dominion of Australia. Rogers knew of the man from his orientation. His official job was assistant secretary to the resident commissioner; his unofficial one was as a lieutenant commander in Naval Intelligence. The New Americans, it had been thought, didn't need to know that.

"Rogers." He confirmed his identity in a prearranged exchange of passwords. "I'm at the Travelers' Rest. There's no indication that anyone has taken any notice of my arrival."

"Good. We were given advance notice of your coming via the courier service, of course." Logan sounded relieved. He hesitated a moment. "We've also been informed of what happened to De Graeff in London—"

"Yes," said Rogers shortly. "And you also know of the evidence he turned up."

"We do... although it seems a bit far-fetched. But we've been expecting your arrival, as have the locals. As you are aware, our policy is to respect their... sensibilities as much as possible. We make it a point not to act on our own here—at least not openly—but to always coordinate with them."

"Right. I understand a New American liaison officer has been assigned to work with me."

"Correct. Grey Goldson, of NAISA—that's the New American Internal Security Agency."

"When do I get to meet this individual?"

"Come to the Residency at two o'clock local time. Don't bother with any special precautions. It's natural for a visiting Imperial subject to come here, for any number of legitimate reasons. Mention your name, and mine; you'll be sent up to the resident commissioner's office. He wants to meet you too."

The restaurant of the Travelers' Rest specialized in seafood, with which New America's seas had been well stocked. After a satisfactory lunch, Rogers drove through the slowly gathering dusk to the Residency, a low-walled compound not far from the waterfront, over which the Union Jack flapped in the ocean breeze. As he approached the gate, he noted that a work crew was whitewashing a portion of the wall that had been spray-painted. They had already covered up most of it, so Rogers couldn't read the spray-painter's message, although he would have been willing to hazard a guess as to its general trend. He left his glide car in the underground car park and ascended to the lobby.

"Robert Rogers, to see Assistant Secretary Logan," he told the (human) receptionist.

"Yes, sir, you're expected." She gave Rogers what seemed to him to be a faintly knowing look. "Take the lift to the top floor. I'll notify Mr. Logan that you're here."

"Thank you." He went to the lift and floated upward until the effect ceased and he need only step out of the tube. A man stepped forward. He did not salute, as they were both in civilian clothes and he wasn't supposed to be military at all. But he observed military courtesy by not offering his hand to a superior officer.

"Commander Rogers? Logan."

Rogers extended his hand. Logan had a stereotypical "Black Irish" look, which was hardly surprising. The reforms that had resolved the First North American Rebellion had included a proviso that no more convicts would be transported to America except by consent of the dominion governments—a consent which had turned out to be very seldom forthcoming. So Australia had taken America's place as a dumping ground for undesirables. A disproportionate number of those undesirables had been Irish, many of them convicted on frankly political charges. This, of course, had been long before Ireland had been granted dominion status, ending the troubles there.

Logan shook the proffered hand. "The resident commissioner is waiting for us, sir. This way." He led the way along a corridor and through outer offices, to an inner sanctum.

Sir Ranjit Tewari was from the Viceroyalty of India. That viceroyalty was something of an anomaly in the Empire, inasmuch as it was not constituted as one or more dominions but was nevertheless internally self-governing—and allotted representation on the Imperial Grand Council—in accordance with a complicated arrangement, which, whatever it lacked in strict logical consistency, was something almost everyone could live with. Tewari was seated at a wide desk, silhouetted against windows overlooking the city. Seated beside the desk was a woman who made a striking contrast to the small dark resident commissioner.

"Commander Rogers," said Tewari, rising courteously, "welcome to New America. Allow me to present Special Agent Grey Goldson of NAISA."

The woman also got to her feet, and offered her hand. "Commander," she said coolly.

"Agent Goldson," said Rogers with a nod. The liaison officer looked to be in her early thirties. (Rogers wondered if she thought of it as her late teens, in terms of this planet's years.) She was tall, slender and very fit-looking. Her straight ash-blond hair was worn in a style whose severity was reflected in her suit. Rogers found himself taking in details of her face, for it was a striking face—strong without being in the least unfeminine, with high cheekbones, a nose with character, and eyes of the sort of light color that can seem green or gray or blue depending on the lighting. Her mouth was wide, and looked like it could be mobile, but at the moment was held in a rather severe line as Rogers shook her hand and felt a not-unexpectedly firm grip. She exuded not hostility but a very controlled reserve.

He wondered what impression she was forming as she gazed back at him. She saw a medium-tall man, spare of build but in very good condition, in his late thirties but looking somewhat older because his thick dark hair was starting to shade into iron-gray around the temples. Aside from a slight network of crow's-feet at the corners of his hazel eyes, his skin was still unlined. His complexion was dark, but he had lost almost all trace of a tan, having spent most of his time lately either in spacecraft or in England (which helped him to blend in on New America, one and a third AU from a relatively UV-poor sun). His features were unremarkable, and his expression gave little away.

With scientific detachment, he evaluated his own reaction to her. He could not honestly deny a tug of sexual attraction. His latest affair, in which he knew perfectly well he should never have allowed himself to become involved—it had been a London socialite he had belatedly recognized as a neurotic twit—had ended in a predictably but disagreeably emotional fashion just before his last off-Earth assignment, and afterwards the Zeta Tucanae system had offered no opportunities for erotic interludes. So, he coldly told himself, he was undoubtedly somewhat vulnerable at the moment, and needed to be on his guard. He could permit himself no fantasizing about Grey Goldson, much less any attempts to turn fantasy into reality. At any rate, he concluded glumly, any such attempts would almost surely be unavailing.

They all sat down and Tewari cleared his throat. "Agent Goldson has been assigned as a liaison officer by the local planetary government." (He carefully didn't say "the *colonial* government.") "She will work with you on your investigation."

"Even though I must say we find it hard to take the idea of Caliphate activity here very seriously," Goldson put in. Her English held a slightly modified North American accent, with even more vowel mergers than the original. "It frankly seems far-fetched."

"Assistant Secretary Logan used exactly the same term," Rogers acknowledged—although, he noted, she compounded it almost into one word, another exaggeration of an American English tendency. "But *someone* evidently takes it very seriously, considering what happened to Adrian de Graeff—and very nearly happened to me—in London."

"Yes, we know about that. But it may have been unrelated to De Graeff's current investigation. As I understand, there's no evidence of any linkage."

"The rather extreme suiciding device implanted in the shooter's head seems to argue against the idea that it was a random act."

"I suppose so," Goldson conceded with no particular good grace. "But the fact remains, we have no Muslim community here for Caliphate subversionists to work within."

Tewari cleared his throat again, as appeared to be an unconscious habit of his. "I should mention that at the moment there is quite a large Caliphate trade mission on this planet. Here in New Philadelphia, in fact. The New American government invited them." He was carefully expressionless.

"Yes, we did." Goldson's voice held just a hint of defensiveness. "Well, after all, the Empire isn't at war with the Caliphate—and New America isn't necessarily involved in the sources of the tense relationship that exists between them and the Empire."

"Of course, of course," Tewari murmured.

And you people just couldn't pass up an opportunity to assert your independence by this little gesture, Rogers thought. *Typical.* "Still," he said out loud, "We ought to look into any possible connection."

"Yes," said Logan. "It's certainly one of the possibilities we'll explore." He seemed to hesitate. "Ah...I'm thinking we might also want to consider the possibility of involvement by the Sons of Arnold."

Goldson grew absolutely expressionless. Tewari frowned, as though distressed that his de facto intelligence officer had raised a sore point. Rogers thought he should speak up, in his capacity as an outsider.

"Yes, I recall reading about them. An extremist organization here on New America that advocates the severing of all ties to the Empire and, eventually, returning to Earth and liberating North America itself—supposing that modern North Americans like myself can be persuaded to *want* to be 'liberated' from the Federal Empire."

"They've never been connected with any criminal activities," Goldson protested. "They're just a debating society."

Why do people always use that term—a "debating society"—for organizations where absolutely no debate about the ideological assumptions is permitted? Rogers decided to keep the rhetorical question to himself.

"Nevertheless," Logan persisted, "We have reason to think there's a faction among them that thinks the leadership is too ineffectual, and favors direct, violent action."

"That's just a figment of the imagination of Imperial security people," said Goldson with what seemed to Rogers to be more heat...and possibly more sincerity. "Oh, maybe there are individuals among them who talk big, but that's all it is: talk." She gave Logan a look that made Rogers wonder if she knew of the assistant secretary's clandestine Naval Intelligence role but had to keep up the official pretense that it had been successfully concealed from her government. "Unless, of course, they're provocateurs."

Tewari went huffily indignant. "I assure you, Agent Goldson, that we would never dream of—"

"Of course not, sir," said Goldson in a tone that neither convinced nor was intended to convince. "I merely suggested a possibility."

"A possibility," said Logan smoothly, "is precisely what it is not." His eyes and Goldson's met. *Yes*, Rogers decided, *they understand each other.*

"Well, Agent Goldson," he said briskly, "since my presence

here is being kept out of the public eye, I suggest that we meet somewhere other than your offices at the NAISA. How about my hotel, tomorrow, to discuss our next move?"

"Yes, that would be satisfactory. Tomorrow at midmorning?"

Rogers agreed, and the conference broke up. As they entered the corridor, Logan murmured in Rogers' ear. "I've dealt with her before. She's really not bad to work with...except at first."

"No doubt." Rogers saw her up ahead, approaching the lift. "Excuse me." He hastened forward to catch her.

"Excuse me, Agent Goldson. It occurs to me, why wait till tomorrow? And besides, I somehow get the impression that we may have gotten off on the wrong foot. Can I buy you drinks and dinner tonight?"

She gave him an appraising look. "Did you have a place in mind?"

"I'm very new here. You'll have to make suggestions."

She seemed to hesitate a moment, then smiled for the first time in their brief acquaintance. It was, he decided, a rather attractive smile. "All right. I'll meet you in the lobby of the Travelers' at six."

CHAPTER FIVE

THE RESTAURANT TO WHICH GREY GOLDSON DROVE THEM, GROgan's Seaview Grill, was well named, for it occupied the penthouse atop one of New Philadelphia's taller buildings, peering out over the roofs and the ocean to the west, where only the afterglow of Tau Ceti was now visible, partly occluded by Eithinoha. The sky was clear, and the stars were coming out in their multitudes. As they sat down at a window-side table, Rogers saw a rather spectacular shooting star, which neither Goldson nor anyone else seemed to notice. By the time they had ordered drinks and were studying the menu, he had glimpsed several smaller ones. After they had ordered dinner, he mentioned it.

"I'm not used to so many shooting stars. On Earth, on a clear night, you generally have to look at a particular patch of sky for a few minutes before you see one."

"It's the debris disk, of course. The Tau Ceti system has more cometary and asteroidal material than Sol by an order of magnitude. And we don't have a big gas-giant planet like Jupiter out there to deflect a lot of the incoming stuff."

"Yes, I know. It certainly makes for quite a show in your sky. But what about asteroids big enough to get through your atmosphere without burning away from friction? On Earth, it's been about sixty million years since a really big asteroid strike—the

one that wiped out the dinosaurs. Does it make you just a little...
well, nervous to live on a planet that can expect that kind of
thing far more frequently?"

"Not really. You're still talking about intervals of time that
are very long on the scale of human lifetimes—or even human
history. I for one refuse to worry about it."

"Still..."

"Naturally we maintain a sky-watch program that can detect
any object that's on a collision course and is large enough to
worry about. And given the Bernheim Drive and antimatter
warheads, it would be simple to intercept it and break it up into
harmless chunks."

"I'm sure the Royal Space Navy would be more than happy
to do that for you," Rogers said drily.

"Just as well," she said with what seemed to Rogers just a slight
drop in temperature, "inasmuch as we're not allowed weapons of
mass destruction—even to use against space rocks."

"Well, that's not all they can be used against." For an instant,
Rogers was afraid he had gone a bit too far and ruined the
atmosphere he had been carefully nurturing. But after only a
second's immobility, her features actually relaxed into a small
smile. Encouraged—and in no immediate hurry to start talking
shop—he decided to venture a little further. "You know, when your
ancestors set out in the early twenty-second century to colonize
this system, they didn't have any of that—reaction drives were all
they had in those days. And they had no reason to think the RSN
would ever be in a position, out there at Washington Station, to
help them. In fact, they were deliberately trying to put themselves
beyond its reach. Seems like they were taking an awful risk."

"They must have thought it was worth it," she said, quietly but
with what Rogers could have sworn was a hint of challenge in her
voice.

Maybe I'd better take up the challenge.

"One wonders why they thought so," he said. She blinked, and he
hurried on before she could respond. "For that matter, one wonders
why the North American rebels of 1776 thought the risk *they* were
taking was worth it. If you think about it, they didn't really have
all that much to complain about. They had the highest standard of
living on the planet. And they were largely self-governing internally,
with colonial legislatures elected by the people."

"'The people' meaning free white male Protestants who met a property qualification," she rejoined.

"Doesn't sound very democratic to us, does it? But the fact is that the colonial legislatures were more representative than the contemporary British House of Commons. And *any* sort of local self-government would have been unthinkable in any of the other European colonies of that era, whose royal governors were absolute despots. And there was never any attempt to impose religious uniformity on all the British colonies; each decided on its own established church, and dissenting churches were allowed to function—something else that would have been unthinkable in, say, the Spanish colonial empire."

"But the British Parliament, where they had no voice, had started imposing direct taxes on them."

"Yes, that was the real problem, wasn't it? Taxation without representation went against the English-speaking grain. That's why the colonists got a lot of sympathy in England—even from the king. But then, William V was a highly intelligent monarch. He wasn't able to avert the whole thing, as might have been easy to do after the repeal of the Stamp Act in 1766. But later, after both sides had gotten a taste of war, he was able, through his political allies, to sell his ideas for imperial reorganization to Parliament—and, with the help of Benjamin Franklin and others, to the Americans as well."

"Most of the Americans," Grey corrected.

"Up to and including George Washington," Rogers reminded her with a smile. "And surely you can see their point. The peace settlement resolved all the real issues: no more direct imperial taxation without colonial consent; the Imperial Grand Council, with American representation, to oversee overall policy; and the colonies reorganized into a smaller number of larger dominions with their own parliaments, and with their borders rationalized."

"Some might wonder if just maybe that reorganization and those border adjustments were intended to dilute the old colonial identities and loyalties." But at that moment their dinners were brought. By the time they had begun to apply themselves to the food, Rogers saw that Grey was giving him an interested look. "You obviously have some knowledge of North American history."

"Some. I've always had an interest in it. And I'm North American myself."

"Yes, you mentioned that before. And I'd already surmised it from your accent—or, as we prefer to think of it, your lack of one." Her smile really was quite attractive, he thought, when she deigned to deploy it. "Also... Well, I couldn't help wondering..."

Rogers laughed. "To answer the question you're trying to frame, my name is not a coincidence. I'm a direct descendant of the famous Robert Rogers—or maybe I should say infamous, considering where I am."

"That may be a bit strong," she said, not very convincingly. "Maybe among some—"

"Like the Sons of Arnold," Rogers finished for her, making his first move to steer the conversation toward his mission.

"Yes, certainly them. But," she added hastily, "as I indicated before, NAISA keeps them under surveillance, and we've never linked them with any criminal activity, no matter how truculent their rhetoric sometimes is."

"But how effective is your surveillance, really? From the reports I've read, you have no idea of the full scope of their membership."

"Well, no," she admitted. "They use all the traditional 'secret society' dodges, including the cell system."

"Besides which, I frankly can't help wondering if NAISA's heart is really in it." Rogers raised a hand, forestalling a defensive reply. "Oh, I don't say that your organization has been infiltrated by the Sons—although the possibility can't be ruled out. I don't even suggest that NAISA personnel are actively sympathetic to them. But the fact is, those personnel are New Americans." *Including you,* he didn't add.

"Most New Americans don't subscribe to the Sons' ideology," she stated stiffly.

"Oh, yes, I'm sure the majority here are as non-ideological as the majority of people everywhere, and that they have better sense than to take seriously the fantasy about returning to Earth and leading a new rebellion that nobody in North America wants." From behind a casual facade, Rogers watched Grey closely for a reaction to this calculated bit of provocation, but saw none. "Still, they don't consider the Sons' message to be beyond the pale, do they? It's just a more extreme form of the version of history they've been brought up on. You might say they lack philosophical antibodies against it."

He expected indignation. What he got was tightly controlled

inscrutability. She tilted her head back and gazed at him. "Why are you so focused on the Sons of Arnold? It seems to me that the Caliphate trade mission that's here would be a more productive source of leads—not that they've given us any reason to suspect that they're up to anything untoward."

"Of course we'll pursue that avenue. But there are limits to the scope of my investigation where they're concerned. They don't have actual diplomatic immunity, but I'll have to tread very lightly to avoid creating any incidents. I need to simultane-ously look into it from the New American angle as well. And the Sons seem the most obvious center of disaffection with the Empire—in fact, it's what they're all about." Rogers cocked an eyebrow. "Unless, that is, you can suggest more likely suspects among the local population."

"Naturally NAISA maintains files on extremist organizations and individuals."

With how much enthusiasm, I wonder? "Naturally," Rogers echoed aloud. "Tomorrow morning, I'd like to go over them with you. And by the way...just remember the unofficial nature of my contact with your agency, and my very presence here. We don't want to alarm the opposition."

"Understood. There won't be any official fanfare when I take you to NAISA headquarters."

They finished their dinner—Grey insisted on paying half—and returned to the street, where her glide car was parked. As it slid through the streets toward Rogers' hotel, he gazed around. Even in the darkness, he noticed things...or, rather, noticed their absence.

"This isn't the way we came," he remarked, as they swung into an empty street.

"No," she said easily. "I decided on second thought that this would be better. Less traffic, and—*uh!*"

They were both thrown forward against their seat belts as the glide car abruptly slammed to a halt. *Tractor beam,* Rogers thought automatically. The focused remote application of gravitics could not only stop cold a relatively low-powered vehicle like this one, it also interfered with the grav repulsion, causing it to shut down with varying degrees of damage. They were immobilized.

Three men ran from a building—presumably the one where the beam generator was concealed. They wore face-covering masks, and they were armed with weapons Rogers immediately recognized in the glow of the streetlights as sonic stunner pistols. Two of them ran to the sides of the glide car and jerked the doors open. "Get out!"

"Who are you?" Rogers demanded. He wanted to delay getting out—avoid it altogether if at all possible.

"No talk! Move!" The man at Rogers' door grabbed him by the upper arm and started to drag him out.

All at once, the scene was bathed in harsh light from above.

About time, thought Rogers as he broke the startled man's hold and twisted his arm around, effectively pinning him to the side of the glide car.

The source of the floodlight—a full-capability aircar—descended, and the faint lines of low-powered laser guide beams seemed to stab the three attackers. Those beams ionized the air and carried electrical charges to their targets. All three slumped, unconscious.

Rogers got out and waved to the aircar. It settled onto the street and a couple of security men from the Residency emerged and loaded the unconscious would-be kidnappers into the aircar. They then entered the building and emerged with a portable tractor beam generator, which they also appropriated. Rogers spoke briefly to the officer in charge, after which the aircar rose back into the night. Rogers turned and saw that Grey was standing beside her glide car. She looked up at the departing aircar, then looked a question at Rogers.

"I left word with Mr. Logan concerning my plans tonight," he explained.

"Lieutenant Commander Logan, you mean," she cut in expressionlessly.

Rogers grinned. "Why am I not surprised that you know that? Well, no point in denying it. I asked him to assign an aircar—stealthed, so as to avoid traffic ordinances—to be my guardian angel, hovering over me at all times by grace of a small signaling device I'm carrying."

"You might have told me," she said as they got back inside and sat down.

"Well...lack of need to know, and all that sort of thing."

"You realize, of course, that your security people have no jurisdiction outside the Residency to make arrests."

Rogers' smile remained in place, but it underwent a qualitative change into blandness. "What arrests? None of this ever happened."

"I see." She folded her arms, right hand under left elbow.

"Your car's grav repulsion should start up again now," Rogers reminded her. "Oh, and by the way, there's one thing that's bothering me..."

"Yes?" Her expressionlessness was absolute.

"How did they know where to set up their little ambush? Especially considering that you changed routes."

"I'm sorry, Commander. It wasn't supposed to be this way." She unfolded her arms. Her right hand was holding a sonic stunner like those of their erstwhile attackers.

Rogers just barely had time to think *Idiot!* at himself before the ultrasonic beam did its work on his nervous system and unconsciousness enveloped him.

CHAPTER SIX

AWAKENING AFTER BEING HIT WITH A SONIC STUNNER WAS ALWAYS accompanied by a splitting headache.

Rogers thought he could remember feeling that headache several times while struggling back into consciousness, before sinking into oblivion once again. It made sense: the effect of a stunner normally didn't last more than twenty minutes or so, and he must have been shot repeatedly to keep him under.

Now, however, the headache didn't go away. He slowly opened his eyes and felt around him, to find that he was lying on a narrow cot in a small, windowless, featureless chamber with two doors, one of which was partially open to reveal elementary sanitary facilities. The lighting was dim, which was probably just as well, given the way even it caused his pain to spike. He blinked several times, and discovered by experiment that he wasn't secured in any way. Ordering himself not to waste mental effort on useless self-reproach, he sat up and carefully swung his legs over the edge of the cot. He reached into a pocket, confirming his assumption that his signaling unit was gone. So—equally as a matter of course—was his communicator. (Whoever had taken it undoubtedly knew he also had an implant communicator in his skull, but they would know that the thing was too short-ranged to be of any use from wherever he now was.) But then he felt in another pocket, and his fingers closed around a perfectly normal-seeming superconductor-loop energy cell such as people routinely carried to provide power for various devices. It was such a standard, harmless piece of personal equipment—everybody had one, all the time—that it had never occurred to his captors to take it from him.

He didn't permit himself to smile, for he had already spotted the video pickup just under the ceiling in a corner of the room.

He gave the pickup an insouciant I'm-awake-now wave.

Presently the door—it was an old-fashioned one—swung open. Two figures entered. One, unsurprisingly, was Grey Goldson. The other was a man of about her age, armed with a stunner. He was holding it at his side rather than aiming it, but Rogers instantly rejected the thought of trying anything, for the man seemed keyed to a high pitch of coiled-spring alertness that somehow went with his general appearance. Medium-tall and rangy, he had a lean, almost bony face topped with thick, curly black hair. He was clean-shaven, but his dark-complexioned face had what looked to be a permanent shadow, and his brows were black. Against that background, his eyes were almost startling in their vivid blueness.

"How are you feeling?" asked Grey.

"You mean aside from a miserable headache?" Rogers sighed. "Still, I suppose I should be thankful that you used a non-lethal weapon."

"Of course. We're not murderers."

"'We' meaning, I presume, the Sons of Arnold?"

Her startlement lasted less than a second. "Yes. I shouldn't be surprised that you've deduced that."

"But your superiors in NAISA haven't," Rogers stated rather than asked. "Must be a bit stressful, leading a double life."

"Sometimes. But it's useful to us to have a member well established in the Agency."

"I can just imagine. But isn't this little escapade going to strip away your cover?"

"It wasn't supposed to. The idea was that we'd both be taken in the ambush and then separated. After which I'd 'escape' and report that I'd been unable to get you out with me."

"But now that the ambushers are in custody at the Residency, won't they reveal you under interrogation?"

"Credit us with a little intelligence. As I told you before, our organization is highly compartmentalized. Those three men know nothing of me. All they knew was that they were going to grab a NAISA agent who was accompanying you."

"I see. But it didn't work out, did it? You and I were last seen, by Imperial security men, free as birds after the ambush was foiled. And now I've vanished. Isn't your role going to be somewhat awkward to explain?"

The man accompanying Grey spoke up for the first time. "We'll think of something." Without actually aiming the stunner, he brought it up into a readier position. "Maybe a second ambush between the first one and your hotel, after your 'guardian angel' was gone. Then we'll be able to revert to the original plan."

Rogers turned to him, one eyebrow raised. "I believe you have me at a disadvantage—in more ways than one."

"This," said Grey, "is Ethan Stark. One of our leaders." She slipped a hand into his free one and leaned against his side.

"Delighted," said Rogers drily. "But to return to the subject: Even if you do come up with some explanation—although this second-ambush story is stretching credulity awfully far—the fact remains that *I* now know about you. So . . . what's to be done with me?"

There was an awkward silence. Grey finally broke it.

"I told you that we're not murderers—"

"Merely kidnappers."

"—and I meant it, damn it!" She drew a breath. "I know we've taken a chance by . . . bringing you here. But we had to do it. Ethan opened my eyes to the reason why. He persuaded me, and together we persuaded the council."

"And as to this 'reason'?"

Stark took a step closer to Rogers, eyes blazing blue fire. "You may as well drop the pretense, Commander Rogers. The *real* reason you were sent here was to investigate—and destroy—our organization!"

"What?" Rogers took a deep breath and made himself speak reasonably. "Look, Agent Goldson knows, even if you don't, that I'm here to follow up leads indicating a possible New American connection with Caliphate activities."

"That's just an excuse! You want to tie the Sons of Arnold to some imaginary Caliphate plot, thus discrediting us and giving the Empire an excuse to take action against us—maybe even with the cooperation of the deluded New American government." Stark's glare intensified, if possible. "Guilt by association—a classic tool of governmental repression!"

"And your fixation on the Sons made it obvious what your real target was," Grey added. "It removed all doubt from my mind that Ethan was right." She gripped Stark's hand more tightly.

Rogers looked from one of them to another and saw that they were beyond the reach of argumentation. "All right," he said calmly. "Assuming your twisted version of reality is correct, we still come back to the original problem. Here I am, I know Grey's secret... and, as you've repeatedly assured me, you're not murderers." *No harm in reminding them of that last part,* he told himself.

"As I told you, we're taking a chance," said Grey. "What we hope to do is—"

Stark's communicator beeped for attention. He listened for a moment, then turned to Grey. "He's here."

Grey went to the door and departed while Stark kept Rogers covered with his stunner. Almost immediately, she returned with an elderly and slightly overweight but healthy-looking gentleman in somewhat old-fashioned clothes. His gray hair had almost completely receded—usually regarded as a sign of lack of vanity, in this age when male-pattern baldness could be corrected by gene therapy—and he had mild brown eyes in a ruddy face. His expression was benign.

Grey spoke. "Allow me to present Dr. Elihu Bricknell, distinguished professor of history at New Philadelphia University...and, less publicly, chairman of our organization's governing council."

"I'm honored," said Rogers, keeping his voice free of irony. *Somebody else's secret I'm not supposed to know,* said an unwelcome voice at the back of his mind.

"The honor is mine, Commander Rogers," said Dr. Bricknell with a gentle smile.

"But to what do I owe the honor?"

Dr. Bricknell turned to Grey. "You haven't told him, Grey?"

"I was just about to, sir." She turned to Rogers. "Commander—"

"Call me Robert. Or even Bob."

"Very well, Robert. We've made you our...involuntary guest because we want you to hear our side. We hope to persuade you of the justice of our cause."

Rogers stared at her. "You expect to turn me?"

Bricknell spoke eagerly. "We only ask that you listen to us with an open mind. Surely that's not too much to ask. After all, you're North American yourself. And your very name reflects a great deal of history."

"Not a history of which I imagine you approve."

The historian smiled. "That was all a long time ago, Commander— I mean, Robert. But Grey tells me you know something of that history. So you surely know what led the Americans of 1776 into rebellion."

"I also know that the majority of them—including most of the rebellion's initial leaders—were reconciled in the end."

"But not altogether. As you know, the Second American Rebellion broke out only a little over seven decades later."

"And *you* know that most Americans were never really all that wholehearted about it, outside of the Dominion of New England. The only reason it lasted as long as it did was that it had Robert E. Lee to lead its forces against dotards like Raglan and clowns like Cardigan. And even he agreed—with visible relief, we're told—to call it off when further Imperial reforms were offered. Those reforms finalized the Grand Council's evolution into a super-legislature for the Empire, in which the dominions were directly represented, with the Viceroyalty still existing within the Imperial structure to deal with specific interdominion matters. In fact he later led the reconquest of the Commonwealth of New England, when it decided it couldn't let well enough."

"Yes," said Stark with a scowl. "He was a traitor—a second Washington."

"But can you really blame him? By the turn of the twentieth century, North America became the Empire's economic and population center of gravity, and the term 'Imperial Federation' was already being used for the Empire's guiding philosophy, which was to eliminate the whole dichotomy between metropolis and colonies. A century after that, when dominion status was extended to England, Scotland and Ireland on exactly the same basis as the overseas dominions, it merely legalized a long-accomplished fact."

"All that is at least arguably true, even though it puts the best possible face on things," Bricknell acknowledged. "But have you considered what was lost—the future that might have been if the American rebels had won their independence? Have you read their Declaration of Independence?"

"Yes, in school. As I recall, it consisted mainly of a list of highly debatable grievances."

"Ah, but the rest of it—especially its sublime preamble!" Bricknell's eyes glowed with visionary fervor. "It expressed the highest ideals which the human mind had yet conceived. It held out the possibility of an entirely fresh start for the human race, purified of all the ancient accretions which the Empire and its associated monarchies have perpetuated."

"But, Doctor, have *you* considered what *would* have been lost? The Empire expanded its power base by transcending the nation-state much as Rome once transcended the city-state. It thus achieved a predominant position that the British Isles alone could never have sustained this long. And it has been a stabilizing force in the world."

"Oh, I don't claim the Empire is altogether evil. But it has held the world back from the utopia which might have been. The Americans, freed from the last rusty chains of European monarchism, would have created a new kind of community, free of corruption, greed and violence. Human nature itself would have been transformed!"

"Uh...are you *quite* sure? I seem to recall some things—such as slavery."

"Slavery lasted until the 1830s in the Empire, but the Americans would have abolished it as soon as they attained independence. They would have *had* to! After all, the Declaration stated quite explicitly that 'all men are created equal.' Perfect equality and brotherhood would have prevailed. And perhaps it still can!"

Idealists! sighed Rogers inwardly. "Doctor, I can't pretend to your academic credentials in history, so I won't dispute any of that. But surely you realize that after the Second Rebellion there were only a few diehards left—your own ancestors. And in the hundred and sixty years since they left Earth, American separatism has entirely died out. From your perspective out here, perhaps you haven't kept abreast of the current climate of opinion on Earth. But the Queen herself is at least a quarter North American—at least the last time anyone figured out the royal family's ancestry. Today, nobody cares anymore. Take my word for it: Today's North Americans don't *want* to be 'liberated' from an Empire which they, with the help of the Indians, largely run."

Stark spoke darkly, in the tone of a man coining a phrase. "They need to have their consciousness raised."

God, thought Rogers, *how did he come up with an expression that stupid and meaningless? Do these people think they're striking a blow for something or other by degrading the English language?*

"We don't expect you to instantly throw off all your conditioning, Robert," said Bricknell soothingly, shushing Stark. "But we hope to at least persuade you that our methods are nonviolent, and that even if—which I do not personally believe—there are people on New America who are involved in machinations by the Caliphate, they are not to be found in the Sons of Arnold. And ultimately, we cherish a hope that you will come to see our viewpoint and become a seed of ideas which may germinate among your fellow North Americans."

Looking at Stark's scowl, Rogers somehow suspected that germination of ideas wasn't exactly what he had in mind. He inconspicuously brushed a hand against the pocket that held his innocent energy cell. No. Stark was altogether too damned alert with his stunner. And even if he succeeded in escaping from this place, he had no idea of where it was, or how to find his way back to the Residency or his hotel, especially given that this was one of New America's all-dark "days."

And besides, he thought, *from every standpoint, maybe my best move just now is to play along—but without overplaying it.*

And, he realized, *I don't really want to hurt these people. Not Grey, anyway.*

He forced a conflicted expression on his features. "Dr. Bricknell, I've never had this expressed to me in these terms before. It's all new to me. Perhaps you have a point. I need to consider these matters—maybe reevaluate my received ideas. And besides...I'm still a little fatigued after my recovery from the stunner."

Stark was a study in skepticism, but Bricknell didn't notice him. "That's wonderful, Robert," he beamed. "And I'm really sorry we had to do that. We'll just leave you alone to think things over for a while."

And so they left it. But the door to his room was still locked.

CHAPTER SEVEN

AN UNCOMMUNICATIVE GUARD BROUGHT ROGERS A FRUGAL MEAL—
bread, cold cuts and tea—but otherwise he was left alone for longer
than he expected. His nerves were beginning to fray around the
edges when the door finally opened to admit Ethan Stark and two
guards, both carrying stunners.

"We've gotten word that there may be a raid on these premises
in a few hours," Stark said without preamble, seemingly making
a conscious effort to keep his voice and expression neutral.

"Evidently Grey isn't your only source of information inside
NAISA," Rogers observed mildly.

"Therefore," Stark continued, ignoring him, "we're evacuating
to other sites. These men will . . . escort you to one of them." He
gave a not altogether convincing smile. "You'll find the quarters
a little less basic there."

"Is Grey coming?"

"Later," said Stark shortly. His tone removed all pretense of
genuineness from his smile. "You needn't concern yourself with
her." He turned on his heel and left.

The two guards ushered Rogers along a corridor and into
the cavernous interior of what was clearly a warehouse of some
kind—apparently a long-abandoned one. The open space was
empty save for a few people, a scattering of boxes and crates,

49

and a small aircar. A door wide enough to pass aircars was open to the night. (A glance at his watch showed Rogers that it was "night" in terms of New America's arbitrary day cycle as well as the planet's rotation around Eithinoha.) The glimpse Rogers got by the Eithinoha-light featured hills and very few buildings, which suggested that they were on the landward fringes of New Philadelphia. So did the vehicle toward which the guards directed him; New Philadelphia, like almost all municipalities in human space, banned full-capability aircars over urbanized areas except for official emergency functions.

"Get in," said one of the guards. Rogers was about to comply when a familiar female voice stopped him.

"Wait!" said Grey Goldson, approaching briskly. She addressed what seemed to be the senior guard. "Jerry, they can use the two of you here for loading. I know it's a change of plans, but I'll take him."

"Uh . . . are you sure?" Jerry looked dubious. "Don't you at least want one of us to come with you?"

"I think it will be all right." She turned to Rogers. "Commander, do I have your word that you won't try any funny business?"

"Robert," he reminded her. "And yes, you do. An aircar aloft isn't the best possible place for funny business. And, as I've said, I want to learn more about you people."

Jerry and his companion still didn't look altogether convinced, but they backed away. Rogers settled into the passenger's seat as Grey lowered the transparent canopy and activated the aircar's grav repulsion. It rose and soared through the door.

As they flew through the night, Rogers' supposition about the warehouse's location was confirmed. The lights of New Philadelphia, fringing the dark harbor, receded below and behind them. Ahead, the hills were in darkness save for the lights of occasional farmsteads. Rogers calculated that Grey was keeping them to a low altitude.

"So," he said after a time, "do I gather that you still haven't come up with a way you can return to your desk at NAISA without a stain on your escutcheon?"

"Actually, we've decided to follow Ethan's plan. My glide car has been left in a location where it's certain to be found soon. Shortly, I'll show up at headquarters, suitably disheveled, and explain that I escaped but was unable to get you out with me."

"I see. And eventually, when you release me..."

"We confidently hope that by that time you'll be willing to cooperate with us and support my story."

Silence fell, as neither of them felt inclined to broach the subject of alternatives. Unconsciously, Rogers reached in his pocket and stroked his energy cell.

"Where are we going now?" he asked after a moment.

"To a farm in the hills that we use as a safe house." Grey sounded grateful for the change of subject. "It's in a largely empty area, but not very far. We'll be there in..." Her voice trailed off and her brow furrowed.

"What's the matter?"

"There's another aircar behind us and to the left." Grey indicated the little rear-view screen. Rogers looked and saw the headlights. "Odd—there shouldn't be any traffic out here at this hour. And he's going awfully fast. And now he seems to be converging with us—almost as though he was on an intercept course."

As she spoke, Rogers saw she was right. He also saw that the headlights were beginning to grow more rapidly.

"The crazy fool—what's he trying to do?" Grey wrenched the aircar to the right, causing Rogers to sag against his safety belt.

But the other aircar matched the movement and drew alongside. By the dim light of its instrument panel, three shadowy figures could be glimpsed under its canopy.

"The whole sky to fly around in, and they crowd us!" Grey waved her arm at the other other aircar's occupants, who presumably could see her as well, gesturing impatiently forward. "Go on ahead, if you're in such a damned hurry!" To emphasize the point, she lowered the aircar's speed.

But the stranger slowed in unison with her, as though flying tight formation.

"Is this bastard insane?" Grey gave another frantic hand signal.

Without warning, the pilot of the mysterious aircar gave it a lateral thrust, and simultaneously dipped to the right so the short stubby airfoils on his starboard side slid under those on Grey's port. Then, before Grey and Rogers could react, he dipped to the left, tipping their aircar over and sending it spinning out of control, downward toward the darkened hills.

Grey and Rogers tumbled about, restrained only by their safety belts, as she fought to regain control and halt the mad spin. She managed to get the aircar righted, but too late to bring it back aloft. They plowed into the ground, skidded for a short distance. By the time they crashed into a tree, they had shed sufficient speed for the collision to leave them shaken but uninjured.

Gasping, Grey shook her head to clear it. "Are these more of your 'guardian angels' from the Residency?" she demanded.

"Spare me your paranoia!" he snapped. "I'm not in the mood for it. And let's get away from here—quickly." He pointed upward. Following his gesture, she looked through the canopy and saw the lights of their attackers, purposefully descending toward them.

Without argument, she raised the canopy and they scrambled out. By the Eithinoha-light they could make out their surroundings reasonably well. They had come down in a more or less level meadow of the low hills. The surrounding area was, if not heavily wooded by the standards of Earth's immemorial forests, fairly thickly grown with trees, which over a century had expanded beyond the confines of the terraforming to spread out in riotous freedom. They sprinted into the shelter of the woods.

These were deciduous trees, clearly in season. Presently the foliage began to close over them, obscuring the light of Eithinoha. After they had stumbled over roots and had their faces swiped by branches a couple of times, Rogers decided to take a chance. He took out his energy cell and pressed an inconspicuous button on its side, causing the plastic at one end to slide back, revealing a crystal lens. Another small manipulation, and the cell became a flashlight.

Even in the dimness, Rogers could see the question on Grey's face.

"A special model, issued to Navy Intelligence agents," he explained. "It has some extra features." Before she could inquire what other "extra features" it possessed, he hurried on. "Unfortunately, it will make it easy for them to spot us, especially if they've got light-gathering optics, as I somehow suspect they do. Let's put as much distance as possible between us and the aircar." As though to emphasize his words, they heard a faint hum from behind as their pursuers landed.

Wordlessly, they fled on through the forest, Rogers holding the energy cell so as to allow only the tiniest beam of light to pass between his fingers. With no conception of any destination, Rogers tried to use the intermittently visible dome of Eithinoha to keep them moving in a straight line instead of circling back. But that was increasingly difficult as the woods thickened and they entered a defile where Eithinoha vanished behind a hill. Rogers resisted the temptation to use more light, which would make them more conspicuous. He was relieved when they emerged from the defile and the light of the primary planet again shone through the leaves.

His relief lasted less than two seconds.

"Halt!" The harsh voice held an accent which Rogers recognized, though it occurred to him that Grey might not. They froze in their tracks. A man stepped from behind a tree into a pool of light whose dimness did not prevent Rogers from recognizing the weapon he was levelling at them: a Gauss needle pistol similar to the Royal Navy's standard-issue Webley. The steel slivers it electromagnetically accelerated to hypersonic speeds were very deadly, especially against unarmored targets. And, to no surprise on Rogers' part, he wore light-intensifying goggles.

They must have planned in advance where they were going to bring us down, flashed through Rogers' mind, *so they could have their friends already present on the ground.*

The question of just exactly how they knew we were going to be flying over that particular ground at this particular time is one I don't exactly have the leisure to consider at the moment.

"And now," the accented voice continued, "we wait until the others have come up. Turn off the flashlight."

"Certainly," said Rogers, and seemed to comply. Instead, he turned the energy cell's flashlight setting up to maximum intensity, and abruptly swung it up to shine in the man's face.

Alone, it would have been irritatingly bright, even dazzling. But the light-gathering optics, which could amplify starlight into something that could be seen by, turned it into a blinding glare.

With a cry, the man brought up his left forearm to shield his eyes and simultaneously opened fire wildly with his needler. The flechettes crackled as they broke the sound barrier. But they were fired blindly, and Rogers crouched under them, crying "Fall flat!" to Grey. Without looking to see if she had done so, he dropped the energy cell and used his bunched legs to propel himself forward, grabbing the wrist of the gun-arm with his left hand and forcing the needler upward. The man's midriff was exposed, and Rogers punched him in the solar plexus with his right fist, a short, hard jab that caused the man to double over with a muffled, wheezing scream. Rogers hit him again, this time in the temple, causing him to collapse limply. Then he turned... and stopped short.

Grey had indeed fallen prone. But now a man was kneeling over her with one knee in the small of her back, holding a needler to the back of her head. A second man held a needler on Rogers, who forced himself to relax into a stance of submission.

"Come," said the man holding Grey, as he stood up and hauled her to her feet. Rogers obeyed, seeming to stumble and momentarily going to his hands and knees. In the process, he was able to inconspicuously scoop up the energy cell (whose flashlight function had automatically cut off as it had hit the ground) and slip it into his pocket.

They were led back through the woods to the meadow where their wrecked aircar lay. The aircar that had brought it down had landed beside it, and as they watched a second one descended. In the glare of its lights, Rogers was able to make out the characteristic Near Eastern features of their captors, who wordlessly bound their wrists behind their backs, blindfolded them, and shoved them into the back seat of the first aircar, which then rose aloft.

"Who are—?" Grey began.

"Shut up, harlot," snarled the driver—almost incomprehensibly, between his accent and the loathing that thickened his voice.

Rogers said nothing. He had made a point, before being blindfolded, of observing the orientation of the aircar as it had rested on the ground. Now, feeling its motion as it made almost a hundred-and-eighty-degree turn and then flew straight and level, he guessed that they were headed back in the general direction of New Philadelphia.

The flight was a short one. As the aircar maneuvered to a landing, Rogers heard sounds that enabled him to hazard a guess as to where they were. Then the aircar settled onto the ground, and they were hauled roughly out and marched into what Rogers could tell was an indoor space. Finally the guards halted them and cut away their blindfolds, revealing the empty interior of what looked like a largish storage closet. Wordlessly, the guards departed, locking the door behind them and leaving the prisoners in darkness, hands still bound.

"Before we landed," said Grey in a steady voice, "I heard grav repulsors that sounded a lot more powerful than an aircar's. I think we're at Patrick Henry Spaceport—probably in a rented aircar hangar."

"I'd reached the same conclusion. By the way," Rogers added with a touch of malice for which he wasn't particularly proud of himself, "do you still think Naval Intelligence is just imagining things—or making things up—about Caliphate activity here on New America?"

It was, he thought, probably just as well that he couldn't see her expression.

CHAPTER EIGHT

THERE WAS BARELY ENOUGH ROOM IN THE CLOSET FOR THEM both to sit on the floor, and with their hands tied behind their backs the wait seemed far longer than it was—an eternity of miserable discomfort.

Finally the door was wrenched open without warning, and even the dim lighting of the passageway outside dazzled their dark-adapted eyes. To Rogers' relief, they were not blindfolded again. But their hands remained bound as they were hauled to their feet and marched along the passageway and into a small, largely bare room apparently intended for use as an office by transient occupants. The look of it tended to confirm Rogers' guess as to where they were; the windows were shuttered, but had they not been he was fairly certain they would have looked out on the apron of Patrick Henry Spaceport.

Behind the nondescript desk that was almost the room's only furnishing sat a man in equally nondescript clothing. His face, on the other hand, was distinctive: lean and dark, with sleek iron-gray hair, a mustache and chin-beard of the same color, and a prominent curved nose. His lips were incongruously full, but held in a straight line whose rigidity was reflected in his eyes. Those were large and dark brown, and behind their studied impassivity a tightly controlled fanaticism almost visibly seethed. As there were no chairs in front of the desk, they stood, with the guards taking up positions behind them, flanking the door.

"I know you," Grey spoke up. "I recognize you from the dossiers on the Caliphate trade mission. You're Abu al-Adel, one of the—"

The man behind the desk gave a gesture, and Grey's voice was suddenly cut off in a gasp of pain as the guard behind her kicked her behind her left knee. She collapsed to the floor as Rogers started to surge forward, straining futilely against his bonds. The other guard grasped him from behind and he subsided, glaring.

"You will remain silent until given leave to speak, as befits a woman," said the seated man in only slightly accented English, sneering as he pronounced the last word. "Especially a woman who is a whore like all Western women." Rogers recalled that even as the rest of Islam had moved away from the religion's traditional misogyny, the Caliphate had reacted by intensifying it. "And while you recognized my face correctly, the name in your dossiers is an assumed one. I am Khalid al-Malani."

"Now that's a name I recognize, from certain other dossiers, although I didn't have a face to put to it," said Rogers. "You're well known in my professional circles as a secret agent of the Caliphate government—an extremely dangerous professional terrorist."

"Terrorist?" The flame that smoldered behind Malani's eyes flared up before being automatically damped back down. "Yes, that's what you like to call warriors of the jihad—the holy war."

"I've been told that's not really what jihad means," said Rogers mildly. "Seems the actual translation is more like 'work for Islam.'"

"And what could be a greater work than the cleansing of Islam and the destruction of unbelievers? We are a purifying force—the successors of the tribesmen of earlier centuries who, time and again, issued forth from the great empty spaces and burned away all the rot and decay of civilization, leaving only the great, austere simplicity of the empty desert and the empty sky."

"The Muslims of the Empire and the Dutch East Indies don't seem eager to be 'purified' by you," Rogers pointed out.

"They are degenerate, like the Moors of Medieval Spain who tolerated Christians and Jews among them. They permit their women to go unveiled. They have been seduced by *shaitan* through your swinish commercial society."

"Too bad you feel that way. Islam traditionally had the right idea about commerce. The Koran explicitly permits trade, and orders fulfillment of contracts, payment of debts, and use of honest weights and measures. It should have; after all, Muhammed was a merchant before he went into the prophet business."

Malani gestured to the guards angrily. Starbursts exploded in Rogers' eyes as a painful impact to the back of his head sent him to the floor. By the time he struggled to his knees without the use of his arms, Malani had come around the desk and was glaring down at him.

"They will be cleansed," Malani continued as though nothing had happened. "But first we must deal with the misbelievers. We will extirpate the Dominion of Israel, that outrage that your Empire has inflicted on *Dar-al-Islam.*"

It was, Rogers recalled, a particularly sore point. Back in the twentieth century the Empire had established a Jewish homeland in Palestine. Its growth had been slow at first, but as the European nations and especially Russia had experienced their periodic spasms of anti-Semitism, immigration had eventually raised the population to the point where it had been granted dominion status.

"Then," Malani went on, his voice taking on almost a crooning quality, "we will go onto exterminate all Jews. And then we will exterminate all Christians, and all Hindu pagans. And then we will exterminate all Muslims who are sunk so deeply in corruption that they do not understand the true meaning of Islam."

"And what is that true meaning?" asked Rogers, shaking his head to clear his vision.

"It can be summed up in one word: *kill.*"

Rogers thought of the energy cell in his pocket. *It might be worth my life to rid the universe of this madman.*

But would it be worth Grey's life as well? And would I have the right to make that decision for her?

In any event, the question was academic, for with his hands bound behind his back he couldn't reach the pocket. All in all, he was glad he didn't have to confront the ethical problem.

"At the moment," said Malani, his voice and entire aspect turning matter-of-fact with the disconcerting abruptness of madness, "we have reason to think we are not secure here. We must move you to a safe place—a place off-planet."

All at once, Rogers' mind became very focused, despite the residual ringing in his ears. "You have some kind of base elsewhere in this system?"

Malani's expression turned to one of self-satisfied slyness. "Certain...allies of ours do."

"Allies? You have allies here in the Tau Ceti system?"

"Oh, yes." Malani was openly gloating now. "You'll be very, very surprised."

"Maybe not as surprised as you think. Are you by any chance talking about the Sons of Arnold?"

"No!" Grey burst out, forgetting Malani's ban of silence. "Impossible!"

Malani frowned at her but did not signal the guards. "Not the organization as a whole. But there is an extreme faction within it, unknown to the leadership. They regard that leadership as a lot of ineffectual old women, and the New American government as little better than collaborationists. They are willing to ally themselves with anyone opposed to the Empire—including us. They are fools, but we find them useful. At least they understand the need for violent action—which makes them willing to cooperate with certain...projects of ours."

"You're lying," Grey blurted recklessly.

"I assure you I'm not. They call themselves the Sons of Wilkinson, after some historical hero of theirs."

"General James Wilkinson," said Grey mechanically. She avoided Rogers' eyes, for she now knew it must be true. Malani wouldn't have been able to make up that name. "He was one of the rebels who refused to give in and follow Washington in accepting the rapprochement of 1778, and helped lead their exodus to French Louisiana."

Thus goes the New American version of history. Even in these circumstances, Rogers couldn't suppress an inner chuckle. *In fact, Wilkinson was a compulsive intriguer who had been trying unsuccessfully to sell his services as a spy to the British—and then, in 1778, sold them out and started offering his services to the French. Washington finally found out what he'd been up to—in addition to assorted cases of bribery and graft—and he decided it was best for his health to join the die-hards who fled to Louisiana. There, he became a secret agent for Spain.*

In short, a treasonous slime mold. These people have no idea of the appropriateness of the name they've chosen for themselves.

Still, he couldn't bring himself to give Grey an I-told-you-so look.

"However, Commander Rogers, you are wrong," Malani resumed. "At present, I am referring to allies far more powerful than the Sons of Wilkinson."

"*Other* allies? And who might those be?"

"Oh, you'll find out soon enough." Malani scowled. "By the way, you have them to thank for the fact that you continue to live, for the present. My personal preference would be to have you flayed and beheaded, and turn this brazen slut over to my men for their amusement before killing her. But they want you delivered to them alive."

Which gives me a pretty good idea of just who the senior partner is here, Rogers thought. *But who can these "allies" be?*

"While we're waiting," Rogers said with careful casualness, "do you plan to feed us? And if so, can we have our hands untied, if only so we can eat?"

"In good time." Malani gestured imperiously, and the guards led them back to the storage closet. There, their bonds were cut away. Before feeling returned to their hands, the door was locked and they were in darkness again, stretching and flexing their stiff arms and sinking to the floor, still cramped but less acutely uncomfortable than before.

After a while, Grey broke the silence.

"Don't say it, Robert. You were right. But I swear I've never heard of these 'Sons of Wilkinson.'"

"I know you haven't."

"But Dr. Bricknell and Ethan and the rest of the leadership of the Sons of Arnold have to be told about this! These crazy extremists will discredit the whole organization. We've got to somehow let them know."

"What's this 'We'? I remind you that I'm not here to keep the image of the Sons of Arnold unsullied. However, I suggest to you that the two of us—you *are* a NAISA officer, after all, and seem to find no incompatibility between that and your Sons of Arnold activities—do have more urgent interests in common. We now know that the Caliphate 'trade mission' is nothing but a Trojan horse for subversionists. We also know that the Sons of Wilkinson are as opposed to the New American government as they are to the Empire, and are willing to help with Malani's violent 'projects.'"

"Yes," she said slowly. "I suppose that does make us allies."

"Furthermore, don't forget these mysterious allies of the Caliphate. I have a feeling they don't exactly have New America's best interests at heart."

"But who can they be?"

"Good question. They can't be anyone local. Someone from outside has secretly established a base in this system. But who would have the resources for something like that? The Spanish Empire? I'm not sure they'd have the capability, and at any rate they're on good terms with us. The Russians? They're no particular friends of the Caliphate, which is always trying to stir up trouble among their Muslim minority. Which to some extent is also true of Greater China, although I'd have to rank it as the most likely candidate." Rogers sighed. "Well, as Malani said, we'll find out who they are soon enough."

"Malani didn't say whether or not the Sons of Wilkinson are aware of them," Grey said thoughtfully—and, Rogers thought, hopefully.

"No, he didn't. But he indicated that the Sons of Wilkinson aren't too particular about their alliances."

Grey had no comment to make. They sat in silent darkness for a time, before water and stale bread was brought to them under the eyes of watchful guards. Another interval of solitude passed. Then they were roused by guards who bound and blindfolded them again and shoved them along the corridor.

CHAPTER NINE

ROGERS DECIDED THAT THEIR BLINDFOLDS WERE MERELY A CASE of their captors' ingrained habit of secrecy about their facility at Patrick Henry Spaceport, doubtless rented through a dummy or a series of dummies. His impression was confirmed when they were guided up what felt like a gangway and presently had the blindfolds cut away to reveal the featureless interior of a typical cargo compartment of a small surface-to-space-capable vessel. Their bonds were also removed, and they were left confined. Both of them surveyed the compartment's bare interior with expert eyes and concluded that there were no surveillance devices. Then, after a short wait, came the sounds and the slight quiver of the grav compensators lifting the ship and the inertial compensators adjusting as the photon thrusters drove them out to where the Bernheim Drive could be activated.

Rogers' guess of how long it would take to reach New America's Primary Limit proved fairly accurate. They felt the subliminal sensation that accompanied the activation of the Bernheim Drive in slower-than-light mode. Beyond this, he could guess no further; he didn't know how many gees of pseudo-acceleration this ship was rated for, nor did he know how far out their destination was.

Grey must have been thinking along similar lines. "If this secret base is in the debris disk, it has to be well outside Tau

Ceti's Secondary Limit. Do you think they'll form the warp field and go faster-than-light?"

"I doubt it. At mere interplanetary distances, they could hardly avoid overshooting their mark. No, we'll get there the slow way." It didn't occur to Rogers to consider what a belly laugh his use of the words "mere" and "slow" would have induced in most human beings throughout history.

"But how can they keep this secret space station secret, shuttling out to it at ordinary in-system velocities?" Grey wondered. "Surely our traffic control—"

"The answer has to be that this ship—which I'm sure is perfectly unremarkable to all outward appearances—has a very up-to-date cloaking field. Same goes for all ships that go anywhere near the base. The station itself won't need one; out there in the debris disk, it's as well-concealed as they could wish."

Afterwards, they could only wait. At least, in a somewhat larger space and with their hands unbound, there wasn't the miserable discomfort of the storage closet. After a time that seemed far longer than it was they began to feel slight vibration as the inertial compensators tried to keep pace with the vagaries of maneuvering thrusters. Presently there was a jar that told Rogers their ship had been taken in hand by a tractor beam, presumably to be drawn slowly through an immaterial atmosphere screen. Then came a bump as the craft settled to a deck. At once, there was a change in weight as the ship's artificial gravity—set at New America's surface pull of 1.19 g—was deactivated and that of the station took hold. It was, to their mild surprise, somewhat higher. Likewise surprisingly, as pressures equalized, the air seemed a little denser than New America's.

After a nerve-stretching wait, the hatch slid open, and stunner-armed guards ushered them out. As they proceeded to the exit ramp, Rogers saw that he had been correct in thinking this ship was outwardly innocuous, for he recognized the interior of a Rover-class boat, about as small as space vessels came—it couldn't have carried much more than themselves, Malani and the guards. He was familiar with the class, and had in fact piloted it. He'd only just had time to make the identification before they came to the outer hatch and the guards prodded them down the ramp.

At once, their eyes took in several things, in no particular order.

They were in a small hangar bay, as Rogers had surmised. The star-strewn blackness of space was visible through the atmosphere screen of pressure-gravity that permitted large slow-moving objects to pass through but not air molecules. But the bulkheads had none of the stark functionality one expected of such a place. Instead, everything seemed ornamented—indeed, over-ornamented, as though someone abhorred blank spaces and felt compelled to fill them in with dense decorative patterns in an unfamiliar, bewildering and somehow disturbing artistic motif.

And standing at the foot of the ramp awaiting them were Khalid al-Malani and...another.

A small scream escaped Grey.

The subject of intelligent life in the universe had always been a contentious one.

Even as humanity was taking its first hesitant steps beyond Earth's atmosphere in the early twenty-first century, the Empire had funded a project to try to detect radio broadcasts from hypothetical technically advanced civilizations. The total failure to detect such broadcasts had led many to conclude that mankind was alone in the galaxy. This, of course, had been a non sequitur, ignoring the fact that radio transmissions propagate at the speed of light, so that a civilization 10,000 light-years away—a tenth of the diameter of the galaxy—could have broadcast them 9,999 years ago without them yet being received. And, at any rate, it had been realized afterwards that the whole thing had been pointless; such transmissions could only get a few light-years before being swallowed up and lost in the galactic "white noise."

And then there had been Featherstone's Paradox: simply stated, "If they're out there, why aren't they here?" Surely, Featherstone had reasoned, if other intelligent races could exist, then over the course of the billions of years of galactic history *one* of them would have colonized the entire galaxy, including Earth. Ergo, humanity must be the only intelligent race that exists or *has ever existed* in the galaxy. A surprisingly long time had passed before Featherstone's Paradox had been subjected to critical analysis, revealing its fallacies. First of all, it assumed an exponential yeast-growth model of population expansion for one species out to infinity—a model that no species on Earth had ever been found to exhibit. Furthermore, it ignored the possibility of there being numerous species existing in their own niches and in some cases competing for various niches, leaving certain "bubbles" ignored. Essentially, Featherstone's had been an overly simplistic visualization of the galaxy's staggering scale, complexity and diversity—understandable, as it *had* to be grossly oversimplified in order for a finite human mind to make any attempt at comprehending it at all.

The Bernheim Drive had not settled the question. A few speech- and tool-using species had been discovered, some of them believed to be more or less equal to *Homo sapiens* in innate intelligence (to the extent that such things could be measured, still a matter of learned dispute), but none were above a Mesolithic technological level. Was civilization a freak? Or could it only rise to a certain level before succumbing to its own malign sociological byproducts, like a fire banked down by its ashes? And if so, why had it arisen and continued to develop on Earth? The controversy continued to rage.

But, thought Rogers in an oddly calm corner of his stunned mind, *I think it's a controversy that has now been settled.*

Malani was not a tall man, but he towered over his companion, who stood less than five feet. "Stood" was the correct word, for he (or she, or it) was an erect biped, and possessed two arms. This was unsurprising. A bilaterally symmetrical vertebrate form, usually with four limbs though occasionally six, had been found to be the pattern on which evolutions generally converged in the case of higher animals; no amorphous jelly-beings or active land-dwelling octopi or the like had yet been discovered.

But this being's general layout was as far as his resemblance to humanity went. (Rogers decided to mentally follow the rule of grammatical construction which held that the masculine gender includes the feminine. The neuter seemed somehow wrong, even though it was impossible to guess as to this race's reproductive patterns.) He was, for his height, disproportionately broad and powerful; the high setting of the artificial gravity must reflect the planetary environment that had produced his race. The legs were short and thick, and Rogers imagined he would walk with a stiff, strutting gait. The hands had four thick digits, all mutually opposable; the arrangement did not suggest great manual dexterity.

The completely hairless skin was a pale grayish cream color, tough and wrinkled and thick-looking. Or at least this was true of the face, which was all that was exposed by a rather elaborate maroon and orange coverall-and-vest garment. But there was one other exposure: the feet were bare. Perhaps, thought Rogers, these beings were vain about their feet. He couldn't imagine why. They resembled an elephant's hooves, with four barely perceptible vestigial toes spaced evenly around the outer edge, reflecting the configuration of the hands.

The face was the worst. A heavy brow hung over deep eye sockets, shadowing the greenish-yellow eyes. There was no nose, just a flat, rather complex breathing orifice above a wide, totally lipless mouth. The ears were likewise flat, and protected by bony ridges. If there was a chin, it was invisible, for the body's impression of stiff squatness was reflected in the domelike head, which rose from the torso with no apparent neck.

It was, of course, impossible to read the face of an unknown species, so Rogers didn't try. It seemed quite expressionless. But then, this didn't seem to be a "mobile face" capable of a very wide range of expressions anyway.

There was one thing of which Rogers was sure. He was familiar with all the tool-using races humanity had encountered so far, and this was not one of them. That would have been certain even without the evidence of this space station.

But, he mentally corrected himself, looking at Malani, *evidently some humans have encountered this race.*

Malani's expression was one of sheer gloating. "You see, Commander? I told you we had allies who would surprise you. Permit me to introduce R'Ghal, a Fifth-Degree Task Leader of the Gharnakh'sha Unity."

"I knew you were mad," said Grey in a tight voice, "but I had no idea how mad. You'd even betray the human species itself, which includes your own people."

Rogers cocked an insolent eyebrow. "What would Allah say?"

Malani's eyes seemed almost to ignite with hate, but R'Ghal's presence clearly restrained him. He spoke in a voice that audibly ground against that restraint. "We must take whatever allies we can find! Your godless, power-monopolizing Empire has left us no other choice. So it's your fault!" He brought himself under control with a visible effort. "At any rate, R'Ghal has assured me that the Gharnakh'sha have seen the justice of our cause, and wish to help us."

"I gather," said Rogers drily, "that you hope to convert them to Islam."

Once again, Malani could be seen to clamp control on himself. But when he spoke, he did so in a level tone. "Our mullahs are still pondering the possibility or . . . appropriateness of what you have, with typical Western flippancy, suggested. But in the meantime, I do not concern myself with such matters. As I have indicated, they are simply allies—extremely useful ones."

"Useful for what?" asked Rogers, trying to keep his voice casual.

Malani hesitated before speaking with an air of boastfulness overcoming caution. "Very well. Why shouldn't you know? After all, you're never going to leave this base alive. We're engaged in a coordinated operation with the Sons of Wilkinson. With their help we're going to seize control of one of your Defiant-class warships."

Rogers tried to hide his shock. The Defiant class was what was called a second-rater, in the terminology the Royal Navy had revived from the age of sail, which made it one of the largest interstellar space warships in existence, exceeded only by the Empire's very rare first-raters and Greater China's gargantuan *Kuan-Ti*. And its weapon and electronic warfare systems were the most advanced in existence. If the Caliphate were to lay its hands on one, intact . . . "And where do you propose to accomplish this?" he asked in a carefully level voice. "There's no such ship in this system."

"I don't believe I'll tell you that," said Malani, caution seeming to creep back. "But once we receive word that it has succeeded, we and the Sons of Wilkinson will commence our part of the operation here."

"Which is . . . ?"

"No, I won't tell you about that either, except to say that the Gharnakh'sha are going to make it possible." With the abrupt mood swing Rogers had come to expect, Malani's reckless bombast returned. "And if we prove ourselves worthy by succeeding in this, they have promised to do even more for us. Something you cannot possibly imagine. Something our dupes of the Sons of Wilkinson know nothing about. Something that will enable us, without further assistance from them, to obliterate all the historical injustices your Empire and the other infidel powers have inflicted on Islam!"

"You," said Grey with dispassionate primness, "are a raving megalomaniac."

"Precisely put," Rogers nodded. "Even if—which I don't for a moment believe—you manage to capture a Defiant and also do whatever it is you plan to do in this system, you can't hope to destroy the Empire, much less all the powers. That's not reality."

Malani's eyes took on a sly twinkle. "Ah, but *which* reality? You see—"

Before Malani could continue, R'Ghal spoke for the first time.

At first Rogers didn't recognize the sound for what it was, because the words were clearly being formed by organs of speech very different from human vocal chords. Rather than the *basso profundo* he'd expected from the Gharnakh's overall appearance— non sequitur though he knew that to be—the voice was a fluting series of guttural cries. But R'Ghal was obviously speaking softly by his own standards, while a kind of large medallion attached to his vest produced a practically realtime translation in pedantic, underemphasized English.

"I believe," said the alien, cutting Malani off, "that no further explanation to these individuals is necessary or desirable at this time. And I would be obliged if they be placed in the detention facility for the present, pending interrogation."

"At once, Task Leader," said Malani, suddenly obsequious. He gestured to the guards.

R'Ghal gave a gesture of his own, and another Gharnakh, in a less elaborately decorated version of the same costume, appeared. R'Ghal addressed him, although the translator medallion picked it up. "Conduct them."

Rogers' eyes narrowed at the sight of the new arrival, who looked astonishingly like R'Ghal. Of course it was to be expected that individual differences among members of a nonhuman race would tend to be outweighed by a common alienness. Still...

Then the guards shoved them forward and the Gharnakh led the way into the bowels of the space station, and Rogers had no leisure to speculate...or to puzzle over Malani's odd final words to them.

CHAPTER TEN

THEY WERE UNCEREMONIOUSLY SHOVED INTO A CELL AND LEFT alone. After they had satisfied themselves that there were no apparent listening devices, Grey spoke. "Have you noticed that all the, uh, Gharnakh'sha seem to look exactly alike?"

"Yes. Including those we saw at work stations as we were being led here. And speaking of those work stations, and also the hangar deck, there's something else I've noticed."

"What's that?"

Rogers paused, seeking to verbalize a general impression. "It's not always easy to tell, under all the ornamentation. But from the look of things, I get the impression that their technology isn't all that impressive."

Grey gave a gesture that took in their surroundings. "This station is pretty impressive, regardless of whether they transported it here in one piece or constructed it in this system clandestinely."

"Oh, yes, they obviously have enormous resources and operate on a large scale. But qualitatively, we haven't seen any indication that they have any capabilities beyond our own. And anyway, I'm talking about sophistication, not scale. The engineering, the controls—everything seems to look kind of bulky, clumsy, and... well, almost old-fashioned."

Grey nodded slowly. "I think I know what you're talking about. But what does it mean?"

"I don't know. We'll just have to wait and—"

At that moment, the door slid open and two Gharnakh'sha stumped in.

One was R'Ghal. The other was obviously a guard. He wore a considerably simpler version of the standard Gharnakh dress, and Rogers thought he could discern subtle individual differences—the facial features seemed somehow cruder. And he carried what was, for all the inevitable differences in something designed to be held in the grapplelike Gharnakh hand, clearly a Gauss needle weapon. This was unsurprising; needlers could be safely used inside space habitats. Equally unsurprising to Rogers was the fact that it was visibly heavier and apparently less efficient than human weapons of the same type.

Of course, he cautioned himself, it still could undoubtedly kill him as dead as he could get.

With seeming nonchalance, he slipped his right hand into his pocket.

R'Ghal spoke, and his medallion provided a flat, emotionless translation that seemed to go with the stolidity of his appearance. "You will be taken to a facility where all useful information you possess will be extracted. Afterwards, Malani wishes to kill you in what I consider an overelaborate way. It is in our interests to keep him content, even though we bear no particular ill will toward you—or, for that matter, toward your Empire."

"Then why are you working with its enemies?" Grey wanted to know. The medallion produced a series of Gharnakh words as she spoke. "And by the way, what is this joint operation that's afoot here in the Tau Ceti system?"

"And," Rogers added, "what's this mysterious thing you've promised to do for the Caliphate if they perform satisfactorily for you?"

"That is all very complicated. And you have no need to know it, nor would you be able to make any use of the information. So now..." He gestured, and the guard stepped forward.

It's now or never, thought Rogers, knowing he could no longer put off playing the one card he held.

With a fluid motion, he drew forth the energy cell that none of his various captors had thought to confiscate, any more than his hair comb. He pointed it at the guard's head and pushed the control button one click beyond the "flashlight" setting.

The energy cell instantly yielded up all the energy stored in its superconductor loop, and that energy gushed forth in the form of a weapon-grade laser pulse. Not a very powerful one, to be sure...but at this range, sufficient to reduce the guard's face to a charred hole. Rogers' supposition that the alien's brain was located behind that face proved correct, for he collapsed, dead before he crumpled to the deck.

Rogers swung the energy cell toward R'Ghal, who flinched back, his normally expressionless face showing what presumably were his race's indicia of terror. The cell could only be used as a weapon once...but R'Ghal didn't know that, and Rogers saw no reason to enlighten him.

He had expected Grey to be momentarily stunned into immobility. But she surprised him by promptly going to one knee and scooping up the needler the guard had dropped. It was weighty, and awkward for human hands, but holding it as best she could she stood up and pointed it at R'Ghal.

"Now I *really* know what you mean about 'extra features,'" she remarked to Rogers with a quick smile.

"So now," said Rogers to R'Ghal in an ironic echo of the alien's own words, "you are going to accompany us to the hangar bay."

"You cannot possibly escape from this station." The translator medallion was incapable of conveying agitation, but Rogers fancied he could detect it in the background alien speech. "If I give the alarm—"

"Then we're doomed. Which means I'll have absolutely nothing to lose by killing you."

R'Ghal took the point. Without further protest on his part, they departed the cell and proceeded along the passageways that Rogers had been careful to memorize. Grey cradled the needler in her arms as inconspicuously as possible, and Rogers, holding the now-useless energy cell to R'Ghal's back, hoped no one would wonder where the guard was. But the few Gharnakh'sha they saw remained absorbed in their own tasks, not noticing the trio's oddities. The same continued to hold true as they entered the hangar bay. The Rover that had brought them was still there; Rogers had had no reason to suppose it would not be, but he heaved an inward sigh of relief.

"You *do* know how to pilot this boat, don't you?" Grey murmured nervously.

"Oh, ye of little faith," Rogers murmured back, nudging R'Ghal forward.

As they neared the ramp, one Gharnakh worker glanced at them, then turned away, then seemed to have second thoughts and glanced again. His expression was of course unreadable to human eyes. But Rogers hurried R'Ghal on, wondering nervously if Gharnakh'sha were given to self-sacrifice.

As they ascended the ramp and started to enter the hatch, it seemed for an instant that R'Ghal, for one, just might be so inclined. He started to turn in the direction of the worker, who was momentarily out of sight behind the hull. Rogers shoved him forward. He had little doubt that this heavy-planet being was stronger than he was, but he caught R'Ghal off balance and sent him tumbling into the Rover.

"Inside, quick!" Rogers snapped to Grey. "And keep him covered with that needler." As she complied, he slapped a control pad on the bulkhead. With a hum, the hatch began to iris shut and the ramp to retract. Leaving Grey to guard their prisoner, he ran through the central cabin, jumped up onto the bridge, and began manipulating controls.

Grav repulsion leveraged artificial gravity fields like this station's just as well as the natural ones of planets. The Rover rose and swung about, pointing its nose at the open end of the hangar bay. In the viewscreen, Rogers saw several Gharnakh'sha in an agitated state whose obviousness transcended species and cultures. But they were unarmed, and seemed unable to cope with the unexpected situation. With a grim smile, he applied lateral thrust, and the Rover slid through the immaterial atmosphere screen. Momentum carried it beyond the negligible gravitational influence of the station's mass, and Rogers activated the Bernheim Drive in slower-than-light mode.

As he did, he glimpsed the station from the outside. Alien construct though it was, he could tell it had been cobbled together out of prefabricated modular segments, which must have simplified the problem of emplacing it in this system. He also noticed unmistakable laser weapon emplacements. At the moment, those weapons were doing nothing; the Gharnakh'sha must rely on their sensor equipment to give them ample warning of any threats, so the unexpectedness of this escape had caught them flat-footed.

(An appropriate image in their case, Rogers couldn't help thinking, with a moment's wry humor.) But he knew he couldn't count
on that state of affairs lasting for long. Without pausing for any
astrogational niceties, he aligned the Rover on the gleam of Tau
Ceti—little more than an extremely bright star at this distance—
and went to moderate acceleration. The station fell rapidly astern
as the powerful though insensible pseudo-thrust drove them on
a sunward course.

After looking over his shoulder and seeing that Grey was
securing R'Ghal in a chair with some kind of cable, he decided
he had the leisure to find out just where they were. He turned
to the astrogation computer and brought up a display of the Tau
Ceti system and all the important objects therein. He expanded
the scale until the blinking light that indicated their position
appeared. They were at a bearing of almost exactly ninety degrees
from Tau Ceti, in terms of the display's arbitrary alignment, at a
distance of about sixteen astronomical units, which put them six
AUs inside the debris disk. The Eithinoha/New America doublet,
following its 1.35 AU orbit around Tau Ceti in a counterclockwise
direction, was at a 275-degree bearing—almost exactly on the
opposite side of the local sun. But Rogers was looking for yet
another icon...yes, there! Washington Station orbited Tau Ceti at
a distance of about thirteen and a half AUs, inside the boundar-
ies of the debris disk but at its "upper" limit in a region fairly
clear of cosmic junk, so the Bernheim Drive could be safely used.
It was currently at approximately a 205-degree bearing, which
put it almost twenty-seven AUs from their present position. Not
particularly convenient, Rogers reflected, but...

Feeling he had put enough distance between them and the
Gharnakh'sha station, he applied full thrust in retro, cancelling
out the pseudovelocity so he could safely disengage the drive, leaving them in free fall at the residual orbital vector of the station.
He then activated the ship's stealth suite, and went down into
the cabin where Grey waited with her captive. R'Ghal was now
immobilized, to Rogers' relief. Given the difficulty Grey must have
had maintaining coverage with the clumsy needler while tying
the bonds, he had worried that the Gharnakh might overpower
her. But R'Ghal seemed not to have resisted. Indeed, had R'Ghal
been a human, Rogers would have sworn that his aspect was one
of apathetic resignation.

As briefly as possible, Rogers told Grey what he had learned about their astrogational situation.

"So," he concluded, "we need to pick a course. In my opinion, our first priority has to be to inform the Navy command that there's an alien base in this system, and that they're in league with the Caliphate to steal a Defiant-class somewhere and do God knows what in this system. Which means we should head for Washington Station rather than New America. It's a pretty long interplanetary distance, but I still don't think I want to try fine-tuning a faster-than-light hop—I'm not *that* good a pilot. Our current free-fall vector is almost perpendicular to the heading we need to get there, so we need to start turning to port and—"

"No," she cut in flatly. "Our first priority is to alert the leadership of the Sons of Arnold—specifically, Ethan Stark."

"*What?*"

"Don't you see, Robert? These 'Sons of Wilkinson' are going to destroy the credibility of the entire organization with their madness. I no longer think it's a plot on the part of the Empire to discredit us—I know better now. But the Sons of Arnold *has* to set its own house in order, and not have the Imperial authorities do it for us."

"But how—?"

"There's a special, very secure frequency by which I can contact Ethan directly. It has to be that way; I can't go through the usual channels, because there's no telling how thoroughly corrupted the organization is. I *know* I can trust Ethan. Anyway, it has to be him. I love and admire Dr. Bricknell, but he's not exactly... Well, let's just say Ethan is more the type for direct action. And he'll unquestioningly believe anything I tell him."

No doubt, thought Rogers drily. He glanced at R'Ghal, wondering what the Gharnakh was making of all this, which his translator medallion was undoubtedly picking up. As always, the alien face was of course unreadable.

"But," he said aloud, "you can't communicate with him now. New America is on the opposite side of Tau Ceti."

"That's why we need to stay on our present course, or maybe even nudge it a little to starboard. It will bring us into a position where New America is out from behind the sun." She gave him a look of great earnestness. "Surely, Robert, you can see why this is right and necessary!"

And, Rogers added mentally, *there's one other little matter: she's got the gun.*

Anyway, there might actually be some points in favor of this course of action. It may put me in a position to learn more about the Sons of Arnold. Especially if I can make her trust me...

Time to put my conscience on temporary stand-down.

"Well, Grey," he made himself say, "I understand your concern. And...I've learned now that I've been wrong about the Sons of Arnold. Don't misunderstand: my primary concern still has to be Imperial security. But now I know it's just the bad apples—the Sons of Wilkinson—that are the threat to the Empire. In fact, I'm beginning to think I can appreciate the organization's ideals. Maybe something of value *was* lost when the First American Rebellion was aborted."

Her look of happiness made him inwardly wince. "Oh, Robert, I *knew* you'd see the truth eventually. Now we're on the same side."

And, for the most part, we really are, he told himself. *For now.*

CHAPTER ELEVEN

ROGERS TOOK THEM ABOVE THE PLANE OF THE DEBRIS DISK, TO avoid encounters with sizeable objects and the attendant ill effects on the drive. Still, it took a while before New America emerged from behind the interference of its sun. Simultaneously, he shaped a course toward New America. When they were inside the debris disk's ill-defined inner edge and about twelve AUs from New America, Grey assured him that Stark would receive her message at such a distance. But, traveling at the speed of light, it would take that message almost a standard hour and a half to reach him. They would, of course, reduce the time required to receive his reply by using that hour and a half to move closer to New America at a pseudo-acceleration that, had it not been "pseudo," would have reduced them to protoplasmic mush. Still...

"Still, it's going to be a longish wait," Rogers told Grey as she settled into the comm station. When she was finished sending a high-security "squirt," he set the autopilot for a sunward course, accelerating without fear now that they were outside the debris disk. "Maybe a little conversation with our guest would help relieve the tedium."

He swiveled a chair to face R'Ghal, who had continued to sit in stolid silence, not evidencing any of the discomfort he must surely be feeling, tied up for so long. Sitting down, Rogers met the pale greenish-yellow eyes. They had no separate irises, but the pupils were round like those of humans, and about the same relative size, from which Rogers inferred a native sunlight of roughly Earthlike intensity. There were lids that served the same function as those of humanity, and R'Ghal blinked them at regular intervals. Rogers could read no expression in those eyes, nor did he expect to.

"I'd like to release you," he said, "but one of us would have to continuously keep you under guard with a weapon, which would be highly inconvenient. And knowing nothing of your culture's concepts of ethics, I wouldn't be able to rely on a promise of good behavior."

R'Ghal said nothing, and his expression did not change in any way Rogers could discern. The alien eyes continued to blink at the same unvarying interval.

"However," he continued, "We might be persuaded to release you temporarily, at intervals, in exchange for information. For example, we'd like very much to know the details of this plan to steal an Imperial Defiant-class warship and turn it over to the Caliphate."

For the first time, the Gharnakh spoke.

"That is a joint operation of the Caliphate and the Sons of Wilkinson. We are not directly involved. I know nothing about it except in the most general terms. So torturing me would gain you no useful information."

"Even if I were in the habit of using torture, which I'm not— or had truth drugs available, which I don't—I wouldn't be able to use either on you because I don't know enough about your race's physiology. In fact, I know nothing whatsoever about it. Or about anything at all concerning the Gharnakh'sha."

"That's right," said Grey, who was standing behind Rogers' chair. "You obviously have the capability of interstellar travel, unlike any other nonhuman race we've encountered, but that's all we know about the Gharnakh'sha Unity, as I believe Malani called it, and we'd like to know a great deal more. We might," she added casually, "untie you while you enlighten us. I'll keep you covered with the needler, of course."

Rogers watched R'Ghal closely for a reaction. As before, there was an odd absence of anything he could recognize as an attitude. The Gharnakh certainly wasn't cringing or cowering; but at the same time, he didn't exude proud defiance. His aspect seemed one of fatalistic acceptance, and Rogers speculated that his cultural background hadn't provided him with particularly deep reserves of resistance to draw on.

For an instant he thought he might have been wrong, for R'Ghal continued to sit like some immovable and unfathomable pagan idol. But then something seemed to sag within the Gharnakh. "All right. Why not? Untie me, and let me stand—sitting in a chair designed for humans is highly unnatural and uncomfortable for us."

Once unbound, R'Ghal stood up with a nonverbal rasping sound that Rogers assumed was his race's version of a sigh. "What do you wish to know about the Gharnakh'sha Unity, which is the closest translation in your language?"

"Everything," said Grey, holding the needler steady on him. "To begin with, where is it?"

"From the standpoint of Earth, it lies in what you refer to as the constellation of Eridanus, so it is farther toward galactic 'south' than this system, and farther out. Its core region is a great deal farther out, although our outermost systems are not very far beyond the periphery of human colonization, as interstellar distances go."

"Outermost systems," Rogers echoed. "That seems to suggest that—"

"Yes. The Unity extends over a considerable volume of space, though not vastly larger than your own sphere."

"It seems an incredible coincidence," Grey mused, "that our races independently reached the same technological level at essentially the same time. You must have discovered the secret of faster-than-light travel only a little earlier than we did."

"No. We discovered it almost ten thousand of your standard Earth years ago. But," R'Ghal continued, ignoring their open-mouthed stares, "we stopped expanding about two hundred years after that. Our frontiers, and our technology, have of course remained unchanged ever since."

"Why 'of course'?" Grey wanted to know.

Even through the filter of the translator medallion, R'Ghal spoke in the manner of one who felt he was being called on to explain what ought to be obvious.

"Because our social system had achieved perfection. Before that, our history had been almost as chaotic and turbulent as yours. Interstellar colonization only made matters worse, for governmental authority could not be maintained across such distances and the stars became an arena of competing sovereignties. Finally, the Unity was created. We turned inward, eliminating all discords and discrepancies, all local peculiarities, all lack of uniformity. Our economy was rationalized into a permanently stable balance. Variations among individuals were smoothed out and leveled, first by regulating which sorts of persons were allowed to reproduce, and later by eliminating genetic variation even among those by substituting cloning for natural reproduction."

Well, now we know why the Gharnakh'sha show such a remarkable resemblance to each other, thought Rogers. *They're mass-produced from a limited number of prototypes.*

"You still haven't explained why the Unity hasn't gone on expanding," said Grey.

"What could be clearer? New technological innovations would introduce unpredictable economic dislocations. New colonies would upset the Unity's delicate political balance, if indeed they did not escape from its authority altogether. In short, society would cease to be perfectly controllable."

"So stasis was imposed on your...utopia."

"Precisely." R'Ghal either failed to recognize Grey's irony or chose to ignore it. "Scientific research was forbidden, as was further colonization and all travel beyond a certain distance from our home system—with the exception of officially sanctioned scouting expeditions."

"Why the exception?"

"The only non-Gharnakh civilizations we had ever encountered were primitive ones. We have carefully kept those isolated and under surveillance, and kept them in their primitive state by whatever means necessary. But the possibility of a technologically advanced civilization was always there."

"Let me guess," said Rogers. "One of those probing expeditions finally did discover such a civilization: us."

"Yes. And your civilization is still expanding; it will inevitably come in contact with ours, sooner rather than later. That is our greatest nightmare, come to life."

"But why?" Grey sounded bewildered. "Why do you assume we'd be hostile? Even if we were, I'm sure we'd be no military threat to you, considering the size of the Unity and our own race's political fragmentation. But in fact, I imagine all we'd want would be trade agreements, cultural exchanges, some form of diplomatic protocols to mediate intercivilization interactions—"

"Don't you see?" As he had once before, Rogers thought he could perceive signs of agitation. "Even with the best of intentions, you couldn't help being disruptive and destabilizing. Contact with you would introduce unorthodox ideas, new perceptions, novel approaches..." R'Ghal trailed to a halt, as though he could not continue because he was staring ultimate horror in the face.

Yes, Rogers wanted to say. *If you let fresh air into a tomb that's been shut too long, the corpse will quickly decompose.* He didn't say it, however, because he didn't want to antagonize R'Ghal and interrupt the flow of information.

"Furthermore," the Gharnakh resumed, "if your intentions were *not* of the best, you would pose more of a danger to us than you suppose. We have had no real war, as opposed to mere police actions, for so long that the entire military mind-set has been forgotten. On the other hand, the very political divisions of which you speak—the pressure of competition between your various nations and empires—has caused your technology to advance at a rate unknown to us since before the formation of the Unity. Our own has been static since then. You, during that same time period, have advanced from the Neolithic to equality with us. You progressed from steam engines to nuclear energy in two hundred of your years, and then to interstellar travel in another two hundred! You have already surpassed us in certain areas—especially that of weaponry. We are making every effort to steal your state-of-the-art technology, but it is very difficult for us to accommodate it in our long-established infrastructure. In the meantime, your advancement shows no signs of slowing. Soon you will leave us far behind."

And you'll never catch up, thought Rogers, *because the whole concept of innovation is forgotten among you, and has been for ten millennia. You no longer know how to go about it. And even if you did, the lack of individual variation among you must smother creativity.*

Anyway, now we know why all your engineering has a slightly backward look to us. Your capabilities in general are still roughly equivalent to ours. But you're right: that won't last.

"So," R'Ghal concluded dispassionately, "you understand why your civilization's existence is intolerable to us. It must be eliminated before it grows completely out of control."

"This is all very interesting," said Rogers, keeping his voice level with difficulty. "Why don't you launch a preemptive war? Nip the problem in the bud, as we say."

"We dare not. For the reasons I have explained, it is doubtful that we could defeat you, despite an enormous preponderance in numbers and resources. I myself don't think we could; the war would only stimulate you to even exceed your already insane pace of technological development. If we had discovered you at an earlier stage of your history, yes, extermination would have been practical...but unfortunately we didn't." R'Ghal was serenely oblivious to the effect of his words on the two humans. "So we must use more indirect methods."

"But you still haven't explained why you're working with the Caliphate. Surely they pose just as much danger of cultural contamination as our Empire does."

"Not really. Their fanatical religious exclusivity serves as a kind of cultural prophylactic. And at any rate, it is clear that the greatest danger comes from your Britannic Federal Empire, because it is the most powerful of Earth's polities and among the most technologically progressive. On the other hand, the Islamic Caliphate has the least potential to threaten us, because of its deep-seated technophobia."

True, Rogers mentally acknowledged. *The Caliphate has always been ambivalent about space travel—something about the difficulty of knowing the exact direction to Mecca. And their warships are less efficient than ours because it seems Allah doesn't approve of direct neural interfacing. And anybody—including their military— who wants to introduce any new innovation has to fight the mullahs tooth and nail for it. You might say it's the Caliphate's one redeeming feature.*

"Therefore," said R'Ghal, derailing Rogers' train of thought, "it is in our interest to promote the Caliphate as Earth's leading power, while undermining the Empire. In addition to perpetuating Earth's political divisions, this should serve to halt your technological progress, or at least so retard it as to give us a chance to overtake it. So we made contact with them...and, through them, with their allies of the Sons of Wilkinson."

"Which leads to the question of what the two of them are up to, with your connivance, here in the Tau Ceti system."

"I ... don't believe I care to reveal that, at least at this time."

Rogers decided not to press the point. He didn't understand why R'Ghal was willing to spill as much information as he already had; in fact, he had been growing increasingly amazed at the Gharnakh's loquacity. But he wasn't complaining, and he didn't want to provoke an adverse reaction. "All right, we'll let that pass for the moment. But perhaps you can clear up something else that's been puzzling me. Why are the Caliphate people so willing to work with you—or *for* you, which I gather is a more accurate description of the relationship? You've already referred to their religious fanaticism, which makes it hard for them even to work with *human* 'infidels.'"

"Well, we have assured them that we have come to see the rightness of their cause, and sympathize with them for the historical injustices they have suffered at the hands of the West, and the Empire in particular, such as the creation of the Dominion of Israel." The translator medallion needed no inflections to convey R'Ghal's cynicism.

"No doubt," said Rogers drily. "And I'm sure they lapped it up. But there must be more to it than that. Malani indicated that you've promised to do something for them, above and beyond making it possible for them to carry out their plan in this system, if they perform satisfactorily. What would that be?"

For a moment, R'Ghal said nothing. When he spoke, Rogers could have sworn—irrational though he knew the impression to be—that the mechanical voice of the translator medallion held a note of amusement.

"All right, I'll tell you. Why not? We have promised to change Earth's history for them, in such a way that things will work out—or, rather, *have* worked out—for what they consider the best."

CHAPTER TWELVE

AT FIRST, THERE WAS NO DOUBT IN ROGERS' MIND: THE "BRAIN" of the translator medallion, however capable it clearly was, had malfunctioned.

"Uh, R'Ghal, would you care to rephrase that? There seems to have been a breakdown in translation."

"I naturally do not know exactly how it came out in your language, but the translation device is extremely sophisticated, and I am sure it conveyed my meaning." This time—although of course there was still absolutely nothing Rogers could put his finger on to account for it—the undertone of amusement was unmistakable. "Even though the statement must have seemed nonsensical to you."

"That's one way to put it."

"So perhaps I should explain. We have assured the Caliphate that we have the ability to travel backwards in time—specifically, the ability to send their agents back to the Earth year that you express as 732 A.D. There, armed with modern weapons, they can change the outcome of the Battle of Tours and enable the Muslims to conquer all of Europe, aborting the birth of your so-called Western culture and eventually converting the entire planet to Islam by force."

Rogers and Grey were without the power of speech.

"We have made clear to them that this temporal transition can only be done with great difficulty and at enormous expense," R'Ghal went on serenely. "Therefore we require recompense for our trouble. They must serve our interests. They are more than willing to do so, considering—"

"Wait a minute! Wait a minute!" blurted Rogers, coming out of shock. "This is ridiculous! It's...it's..." For a moment he was inarticulate in the face of self-evident absurdity. "I hardly even know where to begin. But time travel is a fantasy! It violates the very concept of causality. If Caliphate people go back and change history that much, then the Caliphate as we know it today— including themselves—will never have come into existence. So where would *they* have come from?"

"Oh, we've explained to them that there are no such paradoxes, because any action taken by time travelers creates a new branch of time—an alternate reality. They would be creating one such new universe, and the future of this one would not be affected."

"So what good would it do them?" Rogers spoke mechanically, for he felt a strange sense of detachment from reality, as though he was adrift in a continuum of illogic, calmly carrying on a conversation to which reason no longer applied. "The state of affairs today in *this* universe would be unchanged."

"Yes. But there would be at least *one* universe in which things turned out as they should have. They consider this a worthwhile goal."

Grey, who up to now had neither spoken nor moved, suddenly shook herself violently, as though to clear her head. "This is lunacy!" she exclaimed, clearly resentful—angry, even. "Even if you assume no paradoxes, the whole concept of time travel is absurd for a lot of reasons. What about the law of conservation of matter? You'll have added the mass of the time travelers to the universe centuries early. Also, there's conservation of momentum—I can't even begin to imagine all the ways *that* would be violated."

"And besides," said Rogers, talking over her, "even if this was a theoretical possibility, it's totally beyond the horizons of our technology. How could you have discovered it, when you've admitted that you're no more advanced than us?"

"And then there's relativity," said Grey excitedly. "Any object, or even energy signal, traveling backwards in time would be moving faster than infinity! And don't forget the laws of motion, since motion is bound up with time—"

"Yes." The single syllable from the translator medallion stopped both of them short. R'Ghal spoke on into the silence he had created, in the literal, precise way one adopts when explaining something to those whose intellectual capacity is open to question. "Everything you have said is at least arguably true, in terms of the present scientific understanding of your civilization and ours. Even if time travel is not absolutely impossible, it would require a technology so advanced that it would not seem to us like technology at all. But if you will recall, I have never claimed to be asserting actual facts; I have merely been relating to you what we have told the Caliphate."

"In short," said Grey, staring at him as understanding dawned, "you've been lying to them."

"And they actually believed you?" Rogers was incredulous.

"We were able to fabricate certain evidence, and stage certain demonstrations, that convinced them. In fact, to a large extent I believe they convinced themselves—the prospect is such a very alluring one for them."

"R'Ghal," said Rogers, driven by sheer curiosity to broach a subject he had so far been resolved to avoid, "why are you telling us this? Aren't you afraid we'll tell the Caliphate people that they've been duped?"

"Not at all. In the first place, you are their enemies; they wouldn't believe anything you say, but rather assume you are practicing disinformation on them. In the second place, they would have a perfectly understandable inclination to reject any evidence that exposed them as fools. And finally, there is a characteristic I have noticed in your species—and it really does seem to be a species-wide trait, transcending cultural differences—namely, the willingness to believe things that are palpably not true because you *want* to believe them, and to rationalize away anything to the contrary."

Rogers wanted to dispute that last point. He found he couldn't. The human weakness R'Ghal had identified with such pitiless clarity was one which was frequently exploited in his own line of work.

He cleared his throat. "All right, R'Ghal. But let's go back to the subject of what it is they're helping you do in this system.

You're going to have to reveal it sooner or later, you know. After we make our rendezvous with the Sons of Arnold, our next stop will be Washington Station, where the interrogators will have the equipment to—"

At that moment, the communicator beeped for attention.

Grey rushed to the comm station and busied herself with the equipment while Rogers kept a close eye on R'Ghal. She was at it for a while. Then she turned to Rogers, beaming.

"That was Ethan. He's worried about security if we come to New America to meet him, since we can't be sure how deeply the Sons of Wilkinson have infiltrated the organization. Instead, he proposes that we rendezvous in space. Specifically he suggests that we meet at *Mayflower II*."

It took a moment for the name to register on Rogers. "Oh, yes—the old slower-than-light ship that brought your ancestors to this system."

"Yes. As I'm sure you know, it's been parked in New America's trailing-Trojan position for a century."

"Right—for safety reasons." It all came back to Rogers now. The great interstellar ship's antimatter pion rocket had generated energy by the mutual annihilation of equal quantities of matter and antimatter, and directing the resultant pion particles aft by magnetic fields to produce thrust. Those quantities had been *very* small, so it had been able to sustain acceleration for a long time, gradually building up velocity. The downside had been its more-than-hazardous exhaust: a ravening plume of gamma and other radiation thousands of miles long. Operating it in close proximity to a life-bearing planet had been out of the question. Fortunately, the magnetic sail *Mayflower II* had used to decelerate without the need for consuming reaction mass could also serve as an in-system maneuver drive. Afterwards, since there was no safe way to remove the antimatter core, the ship had been moved to a safe position in the same orbit the Eithinoha/New America pair followed around Tau Ceti, but lagging sixty degrees behind, where she remained to this day, one of a kind. For the Bernheim Drive had been invented even before she had completed her single one-way voyage, so nobody dreamed of building such a monstrosity today.

"That ship is our greatest historic shrine," Grey was saying. "She's always been a major tourist attraction, and school children get taken on field trips there. But she's been off-limits for some time now—again, for safety reasons. A minor instability was detected in the antimatter core, suggesting that the containment field may be malfunctioning, even though it's supposed to be foolproof. Plans for repairs are still in the works. So for now, nobody's aboard her. She'll be a perfect rendezvous point: easy to find, and complete privacy."

"Fine, as long as we don't come too close. Not that I'm a worrier by nature, but—"

"Of course. Ethan says it will take him a little time to arrange for a ship, but he promises to be in the vicinity of *Mayflower II* before we are."

"He should be—from New America, he's got a lot less distance to cover than we do. All right, let's do it. It'll only require a minor course correction on our part." Leaving Grey to watch their prisoner, Rogers went to the bridge, set the course, and reconfirmed the autopilot's command for maximum acceleration. Then he descended to the cabin and faced R'Ghal. "Do I gather that you still don't intend to tell us about what's afoot in this system?" The Gharnakh's only response was a stony silence. "Very well. That can wait until we're done at *Mayflower II* and proceed on to Washington Station. For the moment... it's time to tie you up again."

R'Ghal made no protest. Of course, Rogers told himself, it was pointless to expect an alien to behave as a human would under any given set of circumstances. Still, there was something about the Gharnakh's placid unconcern that seemed unnatural—and vaguely disturbing.

A brief eye-contact with Grey told him she was thinking the same thing.

Stark's vessel turned out to be a Voyager-class utility boat, somewhat larger than their Rover but the same general idea. It grew steadily in the viewscreen as they approached rendezvous.

But Rogers' eyes kept going to the image in a secondary screen, showing at high magnification the spatial landmark toward which both their ships had come, and from which they were prudently keeping their distance. Admittedly, even if the highly improbable worst happened, there was no air to carry a shock wave. Still, a possibly malfunctioning antimatter core could hardly be ignored.

Neither could the ship that held it—a relic of a bygone era, but an amazing one. Humanity's first, last and only slower-than-light interstellar ship.

Mayflower II was very roughly barbell-shaped, and without any familiar object to give a sense of proportion it was impossible to fully grasp her enormous size. It helped to remind oneself that at the front end, just aft of the spherical tank for the liquid hydrogen that was the normal-matter component of the fuel mix, the ring of boxlike structures surrounding the central shaft, seemingly so small, were spin habitats whose rotation simulated gravity by centrifugal force in an era when artificial gravity generators hadn't yet emerged even as a theoretical possibility. Those modules were, Rogers recalled, cleverly designed to assume a slight cant when the drive was in operation, producing a thrust that was long-sustained but too weak to provide the level of acceleration the human body required over the long run. Behind them was the bulge of the ship's stationary hub. Then, farther back along the shaft, came the docking cradles for the orbit-to-surface shuttles: lifting bodies powered by fusion ramjet rockets. Finally, far back at the aft end, there bulked the main drive, including the antimatter containment facilities. Here also were the secondary maneuvering thrusters, and stowage for the giant loop of superconducting wire that was the magnetic sail.

It was a dinosaur nowadays, of course. But it was an awesome dinosaur.

Out of the corner of his eye, Rogers saw Grey gazing raptly at it. He knew that the sight of that ship meant things to her that he could only dimly understand. To her, it was precisely what she had called it—a shrine. But while he would never be able to feel what she was feeling, he could sense the stirrings of an emotion of his own: something resembling reverence for the determination and sheer audacity that had challenged the unthinkable interstellar gulfs armed with technology no more advanced than this.

He forced himself to concentrate on their velocity-matching maneuvers. He brought the Rover into position alongside of the Voyager until the magnetic anchors clanged home and their airlock was sealed to that of the larger vessel. They untied R'Ghal's legs but kept his arms tied behind him and led him to the hatch and into the airlock. Their ears popped as the outer door slid open

and the air pressure equalized. Then, with the inevitable instant
of queasiness that accompanied stepping from one artificial gravity field into another, they entered the Voyager.

The interior was more spacious than theirs, as Rogers had
known it would be. Five men stood awaiting them: Ethan Stark,
flanked by two pairs.

"Ethan!" cried Grey, rushing into his arms. Rogers and R'Ghal
followed.

All at once, Rogers saw Grey's back stiffen, as though her
lover's embrace was somehow wrong. She stepped back a moment,
hands on his shoulders, with a puzzled look. "Ethan . . . ?"

Rogers became aware that the men to either side of him were
suddenly holding sonic stun pistols, which were levelled at him.

With a gasp, Grey recoiled from Stark, who had also drawn
a stunner. Her face was a study in bewildered, uncomprehending hurt.

"Grey, I'm sorry . . . truly sorry."

One of the guards holstered his stunner, drew a knife, and
cut R'Ghal's bonds.

Well, thought Rogers, surprising himself with his calmness, *I
suppose we can stop wondering why R'Ghal was willing to tell us
so much, and seemed so unconcerned about his captivity.*

*He'd heard us talking about where we were going, and who
we were meeting there.*

CHAPTER THIRTEEN

GREY SLUMPED TO THE DECK, SHATTERED, HER EYES VACANT. Stark started to take a step toward her, but the look on her face— or, rather, the absence of one—stopped him. Rogers suspected she was in something resembling a state of shock.

"So," she said to Stark in a dead voice, not looking at him, "you're with the Sons of Wilkinson . . . and you never told me."

"Actually, I'm their leader. And I couldn't tell you, Grey. You can't imagine how much I wanted to. But several times I carefully sounded you out, hoping you could be persuaded to join us. But from everything you said, it was clear I couldn't trust you—you weren't ready to abandon Bricknell and the rest of the old women of both genders who run the Sons of Arnold. They're living in dream world where history is made by rational argumentation and stately position papers. They don't understand that the only thing that can move the mass of people out of their complacent rut is fear—fear of direct, violent action! They talk and talk and talk about their ideals, but they're too soft-headed to kill in the name of those ideals. We're not! We're prepared to use any means necessary."

"Including," said Rogers laconically, "arranging for me and Grey to be captured by Malani, unless I miss my guess."

Grey finally met Stark's eyes, although hers were still expressionless. "So you were willing for me to fall into the hands of Caliphate fanatics?"

"No! You can't believe that, Grey! I love you, and I never intended for you to be taken—that wasn't part of the plan. Not you—just him." Stark jerked his chin in Rogers' direction.

"Yes," said Rogers, nodding. "Everything becomes clear now. You faked that warning of an impending raid, to get everybody evacuated from that warehouse—including me." Stark's silence confirmed it. "And you told Malani where and when to expect the aircar carrying me, so his boys could be lying in wait to bring it down—I'd wondered how he could have known that. All very clever. But then, at the last second, Grey stepped in and took over the job of piloting the aircar." He took on a speculative look. "I imagine the pair who were originally scheduled to go with me in that aircar were ordinary Sons of Arnold members—no need to risk your own boys getting killed in the ambush. Too bad for them, of course. But then, a true revolutionary can't worry his head about the fate of innocent bystanders...which Grey turned out to be."

Stark's pale blue eyes were lambent with hate. "You had to be dealt with. You knew of—or at least strongly suspected—the Caliphate's involvement. That was all you needed. You would have kept digging and digging until you learned—"

"That you were hand in glove with a blood-mad lunatic like Malani," Grey cut in. She got unsteadily to her feet and stared at Stark with eyes that held a turbulent mixture of disillusionment, pain and sheer horror. "You've betrayed all the ideals the Sons of Arnold stand for. We'd never ally ourselves with—"

"That's exactly what I meant! You and the others talk about ideals, but you don't have the moral courage to dirty your hands with the actions required to achieve those ideals in the real world!" Stark took a deep breath and lowered his voice. "Surely, Grey, you can't imagine that I, or any of us, are fond of the Caliphate. But we can't be squeamish about our alliances. We despise Malani and his like—but we still use them."

"I suspect," said Rogers conversationally, "that you're mistaken about just exactly who is using whom. Especially in the case of your *other* allies." He gestured toward R'Ghal, who had continued to stand in inscrutable silence.

"As I've indicated, Rogers, we have to take our allies where we find them. Yes, the Caliphate people introduced us to the Gharnakh, and they've been instrumental in making our plan in this system possible."

"I've been a bit curious about that plan," said Rogers, doing his best to make his curiosity sound mild. "We know from Malani that you're planning to somehow take control of an Imperial Defiant-class warship somewhere else and turn it over to the Caliphate."

"Yes. It's how we're repaying them for their help here in the Tau Ceti system. Our operation here will commence shortly after the seizure of the Defiant is scheduled to take place—and we'll go ahead whether that succeeds or not."

"Go ahead with what?" Rogers continued to try to give the impression of only casual interest.

For a moment, Stark looked conflicted. Rogers suspected that his habit of secrecy was warring with his desire to impress someone other than his own underlings. Then Stark grinned in a way that told Rogers the latter had won.

"I can tell you that it's going to come as quite a surprise to you Imperials, because you've denied us New Americans weapons of mass destruction. But all the while, it's never occurred to you that we're sitting on top of such a weapon—a very impressive one. You never thought of it because it's so obvious." Stark waved theatrically in the direction of a viewscreen that showed a magnified image of the *Mayflower II* much like the one Rogers had been watching earlier.

Rogers and Grey exchanged an uncomprehending look.

"Do you have any idea of the destructive power of that antimatter pion rocket?" Stark resumed. "Its exhaust is like an incredibly powerful particle-beam weapon with a range of thousands of miles."

"But," said Grey, perplexed, "nobody's aboard her. And the rocket's not operational. And anyway, what could it be used against, out here in deep space? That's precisely why she's parked in this orbit."

"You only think she's deserted, and that the drive doesn't work," said Stark with a self-satisfied smirk. "That 'malfunction of the antimatter core's containment field' was a hoax engineered by us, to get the ship evacuated. Now *we're* aboard her. So are some Caliphate people. They've provided something we lacked: the technical expertise to get the pion rocket working again." He paused theatrically. "We're going to use that rocket to destroy Washington Station!"

For a couple of heartbeats there was dead silence. Rogers shattered it with a whoop of laughter.

"Stark, in addition to being a lying, ruthless zealot, you're a bloody lunatic! Washington Station is—what? About fourteen astronomical units from here? And that's straight-line distance, not the matching orbit *Mayflower II* would have to follow, regardless of whether you use the pion rocket or the magnetic sail. That ancient clunker would take forever to get there! Under Bernheim Drive, Navy ships could intercept and disable her at their leisure, a dozen times over. Remember, she's unarmed unless you count the pion rocket—and she'd be too clumsy to use that against moving targets."

"Ah, but that's where our friends the Gharnakh'sha come in." Stark was openly gloating now. "They've fitted *Mayflower II* with a Bernheim Drive—although of course they don't call it that. A very weak one: The maximum pseudovelocity is just under a hundred times the speed of light. But that's all right. It will take only about a minute and a quarter to cover a distance of fourteen AUs. In fact, it will have to be very precisely calculated so as not to overshoot the target."

"You're going translight? But you'd be trying to form the warp field inside Tau Ceti's Secondary Limit."

"Just barely inside. Remember, Tau Ceti is a less massive star than Sol, with a lower gravity. However, you're basically correct: Even though we won't have to shed any pseudovelocity at the end of the hop—merely disengaging the warp field does that, in faster-than-light mode—the Bernheim Drive will undoubtedly be wrecked beyond repair. But that's all right too, for that one jump is all that's required of it. *Mayflower II* will seem to simply vanish from its present orbit. A minute and a quarter later, while everyone is still in shock and trying to figure out what could have happened, it will reappear in the vicinity of Washington Station. The people there will be dead before they realize what's happening. The very ship that brought our ancestors to this system will be the instrument of our liberation!

"Once the people of New America learn that the Imperial military presence in this system no longer exists, they'll know that the Empire is not invincible." Stark had passed beyond gloating; now he was raving. "And the leaders of the Sons of Arnold will realize that we of the Sons of Wilkinson have been right all along. Under our leadership, New America will rise in rebellion against the fictional quasi-autonomy that now masks its servitude, and declare total independence! And on Earth, when the people of North America hear the news, they will be inspired to throw off the shackles they have borne for five hundred years!"

Grey's mouth hung open as she stared at someone she had thought she had known, and loved.

Rogers turned and faced R'Ghal. The Gharnakh had never looked more alien.

"You do realize he's mad, don't you?" asked Rogers, knowing full well the question's futility.

The translator medallion somehow conveyed the bland smoothness of R'Ghal's reply. "We have come to understand the great historical injustice against which the Sons of Wilkinson are struggling, and have willingly offered to help them in their glorious, heroic fight for liberation."

"Well," breathed Rogers, "I would never have thought it possible, but it seems we've discovered a race that exceeds the capacity of *Homo sapiens* for hypocrisy."

"And that's not all," Stark resumed, showing no sign of having noticed the exchange, wrought up as he was in his own rhetoric. "The Gharnakh'sha are going to enable us to actually show our people what the world should have been like—what it *would* have been like but for traitors like Washington and Adams and Franklin! Tell him, R'Ghal!"

By now, Rogers was confident of his ability to detect the indefinable flicker of amusement in those alien eyes. It was in full force now, although of course the translator medallion reflected none of it.

"We are able, with great difficulty, to travel backwards in time and, by altering the past, create alternate timelines. Out of our great sympathy for the Sons of Wilkinson, we have agreed to send their agents back to your Earth year 1778, where they will perform certain assassinations—including the three individuals just mentioned—in such a way as to make it appear the British Crown is responsible. This will decapitate the leadership of the peace effort, and infuriate the Americans so that they will fight on under Arnold and win their independence."

"And afterwards," Stark cut in, unable to restrain himself, "we'll take people back to various later periods in that timeline—the twentieth and twenty-first centuries, say—so they can see the world of peace and perfect equality in those centuries that will have resulted. So in addition to having created such a universe, we will be able to use it as an example to motivate today's North Americans in ours."

"It may surprise you to learn that R'Ghal has made exactly the same bogus promise to the Caliphate," said Rogers quietly.

Stark's expression abruptly changed to one of almost boyish pleasure at his own cleverness. "Oh, I know that. Malani's the one who's in for a surprise. He doesn't know that R'Ghal is lying to him. It's *our* cause that the Gharnakh'sha have embraced!"

Rogers looked from Stark to R'Ghal and back again. He started to open his mouth, but then just shook his head. *If I weren't a prisoner of armed extremists,* he thought, *this would be just too funny.*

"But Ethan," said Grey in a voice charged with desperation, "you're wrong! R'Ghal is lying to both of you! Time travel is impossible—R'Ghal has admitted it to us."

"No!" Stark shook his head repeatedly and almost violently. "You're wrong. We've seen proof. And of course an advanced civilization like the Gharnakh'sha would *have* to favor us—the party of progress—and not a bunch of reactionaries like the Caliphate."

Had R'Ghal been a human, Rogers would have sworn that the Gharnakh was giving him an I-told-you-so look.

"Ethan, you've got to listen to me!" said Grey pleadingly. "The Gharnakh'sha don't care a damn about you or Malani or your causes. They're just using both of you. All they want is to undermine the Empire, while building up the Caliphate because they see it as a lesser threat to them."

"Even if that were true... well, if they want to tear down the Empire, hooray for them!"

"You'd prefer the Caliphate as the dominant power?"

"*Anything* would be better than the damned Empire!" Stark's eyes blazed with fanaticism.

"Ethan, you know there's a lot I don't like about the Empire. But... the Caliphate? Whatever differences we have with the Empire are pretty trivial by comparison." She approached Stark, put her hands on his shoulders, and spoke, a cry from the heart. "Ethan, darling, please come back to me!"

Gently but firmly, Stark took her wrists and removed her hands from him. His expression, it seemed to Rogers, was one of sadness.

"I'm sorry, Grey. It's clear to me now: You've been corrupted—by him." Stark gave Rogers a quick glare. "I can no longer trust you. I'm letting R'Ghal take both of you back to the Gharnakh station in the Rover."

"Are you unaware that before we escaped, R'Ghal was about to turn Grey over to Malani and his boys to have fun with?" asked Rogers. "Or do you just not give a damn?"

Stark flushed. He turned to the Gharnakh. "R'Ghal, I want your promise that you won't let Malani harm Grey."

"Of course."

Stark turned to one of his men—a husky blond youngster in his early to mid twenties. "Colin, go with them. R'Ghal can pilot, but he'll need someone to guard them. For now, take them back aboard the Rover and secure them. I've got some business with R'Ghal before you depart, after which I'll be returning to New America."

Grey and Colin made eye contact, in a way that suggested to Rogers that they knew each other.

"Right," said Colin, not sounding very enthusiastic. He gestured with his stunner toward the hatch.

Grey turned back to Stark and tried to hold his eyes. "Ethan..." she began in a small voice.

But Stark turned away. Colin gestured again and herded them through the airlock.

CHAPTER FOURTEEN

IT WAS ALMOST A HOMECOMING OF SORTS. A SUBDUED COLIN left Rogers and Grey in the same cargo compartment they had been confined in before. And, also as before, they could talk freely in the absence of audio pickups.

Nevertheless, Rogers felt no inclination to intrude on Grey's silent misery.

She slumped into a corner and sat on the deck, hugging her knees and staring at nothing. Rogers sat as far from her as the cramped space permitted and did not try to meet her eyes.

After a while, she shifted position and looked at him. Her expression was no longer vacant. Nor was it grieving. Instead, it held a bleakness that startled him. It said that there would be time for tears later.

"You were right about everything," she stated flatly, without preamble.

This, Rogers thought, was not the time to rub anything in. "It came as a surprise to me too, about Stark," he offered cautiously.

She winced slightly at the name of her former lover, but her features immediately smoothed themselves out and she continued in a tone of grim resolve, speaking at least as much to herself as to him. "So there's only one thing to do. And it has to be done."

"What's that?" he asked, puzzled.

She did not answer him directly. Instead, she met his eyes

and spoke in a sternly controlled voice. "Just don't be surprised at anything that happens. And don't interfere. You can use your judgment about playing along, but be cautious."

Rogers stared. This was a Grey Goldson he had never seen before—an altogether more formidable one. But, he realized, it wasn't new. It had been there all along. Something had now been burned away to reveal it.

Before he could ask her to be a little more specific, the door slid open and Colin entered with two standard ration cartons in his left hand. His right hand held his stunner, with which he kept the prisoners covered, but in what seemed to Rogers a rather unenthusiastic, even desultory way. He considered attempting to jump the youthful guard, but decided against in view of Grey's last, enigmatic words. And anyway, Colin was younger, larger, and (as a native of a 1.19 g planet) almost certainly stronger than he.

"It may be a while before R'Ghal comes aboard and we can leave," said Colin, making an effort at gruffness that fell flat. If anything, he sounded almost apologetic. "I thought you two could probably use something to eat—I don't know how long it will be before you get another chance."

"Why, thank you, Colin!" said Grey. Rogers had to command himself not to gawk, for she had accomplished a remarkable transformation in mere seconds. Her voice was low, husky, almost caressing. And her smile, which he had always thought quite attractive at its infrequent best, was now positively lovely. "That's very thoughtful...but then, that's the Colin Forbes I remember."

Colin blushed and mumbled something. Rogers decided his earlier supposition that these two knew each other within the relatively small family of the Sons of Arnold had been correct.

"How have you been?" Grey went on. "I haven't seen much of you in quite a while...though not by choice."

Colin's fair cheeks grew redder. "I've been fine. No news, except...well..." He trailed to a miserably embarrassed halt.

"Except your involvement with the Sons of Wilkinson," Grey finished for him. Her tone was not accusatory. Indeed, it was almost teasing.

"Er...well, of course I couldn't tell you..."

"Of course not. Although, the few times I've seen you lately, I've noticed you seemed to be sort of distracted and tense." Grey frowned. "I've seen the same thing in Ethan—only more so. I think that's part of the reason why he and I . . . well, it just hasn't been the same with us anymore."

Something awoke in Colin's eyes. His entire aspect spoke of long-term, hopeless infatuation which had suddenly and unexpectedly glimpsed a flicker of hope.

"I guess that's why I've found myself thinking more and more of you, Colin," Grey went on in a soft voice. "Or one of the reasons."

Colin tried to speak, but his tongue failed him.

All at once, Rogers understood what Grey had meant about something that had to be done. And he recognized the hypocrisy of his own feelings about it.

Colin, who had let the stunner waver away from Rogers, now brought it abruptly back on line and gave him a look compounded of hostility and embarrassment. Rogers made himself slump in a dejected way and give Colin a negligent wave.

"Don't mind me," he said, putting a kind of defeated surliness into his voice. "Go ahead. I've never liked her all that much anyway." He turned away, registering a case of the sulks.

"Colin," said Grey, with urgency entering her voice, "you know what Malani was going to do to me—and what he'll do now, once you take me back aboard the Gharnakh station."

Colin blinked as though he had been struck. "No! You heard Ethan—he made R'Ghal promise no harm would come to you."

"R'Ghal is an alien. What do his promises to a human mean? And besides, he has a vested interest in keeping Malani happy and content. I mean nothing to him."

Sweat popped out on Colin's brow, and he wet his lips.

"You won't let anything like that happen to me, will you, Colin?" Grey's voice was both piteous and seductive.

"I swear I won't, Grey! I'll protect you!"

"I know you will, Colin," she said softly. With a smile, she rose and went to him.

Colin was visibly quivering with eagerness to take her in his arms, but his glance—and his stunner—kept going toward Rogers, who was concentrating on maintaining his air of cynical unconcern.

"Isn't there somewhere we can go?" Grey asked. "Somewhere private?"

"Sure," Colin blurted. "R'Ghal probably won't be aboard for a while. Come on."

They departed, and were gone for a long time. Rogers made

himself as comfortable as possible and amused himself with pleasurable thoughts of what he would do to Ethan Stark when the opportunity arose.

When they returned, they both seemed out of breath—and, Rogers thought, not just for the expected reason.

"R'Ghal is back aboard sooner than expected," Grey gasped. "We were lucky to get back here just before he boarded."

"And he wants to leave right now," Colin added grimly. "Ethan and the others are going back to New America."

Even as he spoke, they could feel the slight vibration as the two vessels' airlocks unsealed from each other and the inertial compensators adjusted as the maneuvering thrusters eased them apart. Presently came the faint hum as the Rover went into sublight-mode Bernheim Drive.

"Colin, darling," said Grey urgently, "now we're on our way to the Gharnakh station—and Malani. You know what that means. You can't let us arrive there."

Colin's youthful face was a study in torment. "But Ethan ordered me to take you there. I can't betray him!"

"Colin, remember what we were just talking about, between—" She glanced at Rogers and left it at that. "Ethan's plan can't succeed. You know that. And even if it did, it would only benefit the Caliphate and the Gharnakh."

"Yes, you've made me understand that. But...where can we go?"

"Washington Station."

"Washington Station? But—"

"Yes. If we give the Imperial authorities warning, they can stop this madness before it goes too far, while there's still hope for Ethan. We have to save him from himself." Grey spoke with great earnestness. "I still have enough feelings left for Ethan that I wouldn't let him suffer for his mistake. I'd use my position in NAISA to help shield him from punishment."

She's lying, of course, Rogers told himself. *At least I* hope *she's lying.*

And even if she's not, I most certainly can let him suffer.

"That's right, Colin," he said, hoping his contribution wouldn't be counterproductive. "As I've told Grey, I've come to see that there may be some justice in the Sons of Arnold's cause. I'll also use my influence on Ethan's behalf. And, of course, yours."

Colin was still in a visible agony of indecision. Grey took his hands in hers, held his eyes, and smiled a tremulous smile. "Remember, Colin, you promised you'd protect me."

That did it. Colin still didn't look happy, but all doubts were resolved. He gripped Grey's hands tightly and swallowed hard. "Yes! I'll take control of the ship."

Women! sighed Rogers mentally. Not, he admitted to himself, that he was in a position to complain.

"Just one thing," he cautioned. "Does that stun pistol of yours have the same effect on the Gharnakh nervous system?"

"I don't know," Colin admitted. "The question has never come up before."

"Then we'll just have to be prepared for all eventualities. Let's go."

The cargo compartment was aft of the central cabin. They emerged stealthily and looked down the cabin's length. At the forward end was the raised bridge. R'Ghal was seated (uncomfortably, it seemed, in a human-configured chair) with his back to them, occupied with the controls. They advanced until they were only a few wards from the bridge. Somewhat unsteadily, Colin raised his stunner and pointed it at the Gharnakh.

"Stand up slowly and turn around, with your hands visible," he called out, his voice barely quavering.

R'Ghal obeyed, moving with his customary deliberation. As usual, his expression was unreadable.

"What is the meaning of this?"

"I'm taking command of this vessel." Colin's voice had firmed up.

"What are your intentions? Would you betray your cause?"

"That's not your concern. We're going to have to confine you. If you cooperate, I won't be forced to stun you."

"Very well. I won't resist."

"I'll go up and get him," said Rogers, moving toward the short ladder to the side of the bridge. Colin relaxed somewhat and partially lowered the stunner.

With a motion whose swiftness seemed surprising in such a squat being (non sequitur though Rogers knew that to be), R'Ghal's hand darted behind him, then swept around, holding a Gharnakh-designed Gauss needler. There was a vicious rapid-fire snapping sound as a stream of little steel slivers broke the sound barrier. Blood sprayed from a row of tiny holes in Colin's back. Grey screamed.

With the same unexpected speed, R'Ghal swung the needler around toward Rogers, who had just reached the top of the ladder and was too close to miss.

Even as Colin sank to the deck, he managed to get off a shot with his stunner.

It was at once demonstrated that the sonic stunner did not induce instantaneous unconsciousness in the Gharnakh'sha as it did in humans. But R'Ghal staggered, and his motion suddenly grew sluggish.

It gave Rogers time to bound up onto the bridge and across the few feet separating them. He crashed into R'Ghal, gripping the hand holding the needler and twisting the weapon between them as they grappled. They struggled chest to chest, and Rogers could smell the strangeness of Gharnakh breath.

The high-gravity-evolved being was as strong as Rogers had expected. But his arm was in an awkward position, with the needler pressed into his own midriff. Before he could wrench it around by sheer force, Rogers frantically pushed and prodded with his fingers at anything that would move on the unfamiliar weapon. All at once, there was a muffled staccato sound as it spat flechettes into R'Ghal. The alien convulsed and stiffened, emitting a desolate sound which the medallion did not translate, and Rogers found himself clutching a heavy load of dead weight. The Gharnakh'sha, he decided, died more neatly than humans, or at least more odorlessly.

Lowering the alien carcass to the deck, Rogers went down to the cabin, where Colin Forbes lay on his back in a spreading pool of blood. Grey knelt over him.

"I'm sorry, Colin. I'm so sorry."

Rogers doubted if the dying young man understood the full meaning of what it was she was sorry for. Colin tried to speak, but only brought a bloody foam to his mouth.

Grey leaned down and placed a gentle kiss on his forehead. He managed to smile. Then the stench of human death filled the cabin.

Grey stood up. Her face was a frozen mask through which no emotions were allowed to be glimpsed.

"Well," she said tonelessly, "let's get going to Washington Station."

"Right. And en route, we can spend our time coming up with a story to account for my original capture without revealing your role in it—or your membership in the Sons of Arnold."

CHAPTER FIFTEEN

CAPTAIN ARTHUR VIGLIONE, RSN, WAS A NORTH AMERICAN, FROM the Dominion of New England to which so many of New America's people traced their ancestry. It had been thought that his appointment as commanding officer of Washington Station and therefore senior Imperial naval officer in the Tau Ceti system might have a reconciling effect. The results had been mixed. And at any rate, he was seldom present on New America, but spent most of his time aboard the station, where he was currently.

"Yes, Commander Rogers, of course we heard of the attempt—the seemingly unsuccessful attempt—to abduct you and Agent Goldson, followed by your disappearance." He gazed across his desk at Rogers and Grey with sharp dark eyes. "It would seem that the kidnappers had a second string to their bow."

"Correct, Captain. After the security men returned to the Residency with their prisoners, leaving me and Agent Goldson alone, another group of assailants who had been waiting in reserve appeared and captured us." Ironically enough, they had decided to use Stark's idea for an explanation that would conceal Grey's involvement. "We were held in a warehouse used by the Sons of Arnold, but as we later found out our abduction was the work of the clandestine extremist group the Sons of Wilkinson, without the knowledge of the mainstream organization." This last bit of prevarication was one on which Grey had insisted. "Afterward, a false warning of a raid planted by the Sons of Wilkinson caused the warehouse to be evacuated." Rogers' lapse into truthfulness didn't last. "A member of the Sons of Wilkinson took the two of us off in an aircar and turned us over to their Caliphate allies."

"An alliance of which you've assured me the leadership of the Sons of Arnold are unaware."

"Yes, sir," said Rogers, relieved to be back in the realm of truth for a bit. "Subsequently, the Caliphate people took us to the Gharnakh station."

"Ah, yes...the Gharnakh'sha." Viglione grew grim indeed. He had seen R'Ghal's corpse—the incontrovertible piece of evidence that caused him to unreservedly accept the rest of the story.

Rogers proceeded to give a factual account of their escape from the Gharnakh station. Viglione's frown deepened into a scowl. "But after that, why did you go to the *Mayflower II*? Why didn't you come straight here?"

Rogers and Grey exchanged a fleeting corner-of-the-eyes glance. This was the most awkward part, calling for the most creative lying. Rogers put on a sheepish expression.

"Well, Captain, this is very embarrassing—humiliating, actually. But the fact of the matter is, R'Ghal got the drop on us with a Gauss needle weapon and locked us up. I blame myself for carelessness and cockiness."

"No, we were both to blame," Grey insisted with every appearance of sincerity.

Viglione looked from one of them to the other with his disconcertingly sharp gaze, but did not pursue the matter. *He probably thinks nobody would make such an admission unless it was inescapably true*, Rogers decided.

"But," the captain persisted, "having recaptured you, why didn't R'Ghal simply take you back to the Gharnakh station?"

It's a good thing Grey and I took the trouble to work out this story in detail, Rogers told himself. *The good captain is altogether too bloody smart.*

"As we found out later, R'Ghal had been planning to go to *Mayflower II* anyway, for a meeting with his Sons of Wilkinson allies. So, after letting his people—I suppose the word is permissible—know he was back in control of the situation, he decided to continue on. Grey and I were just along for the ride."

"It's fortunate you were," said Viglione drily, "considering some of the things you've told me you found out as a result."

"Indeed, sir. It was at the rendezvous near *Mayflower II* that we learned of the double game the Gharnakh are playing with the Caliphate and the Sons of Wilkinson."

"Yes, the time-travel hoax," Viglione nodded sourly.

"It was also there that Ethan Stark—who we learned is the leader of the Sons of Wilkinson—told us about their plans. Afterwards, at the same time he returned to New America, he let R'Ghal take us back to the Gharnakh station, along with a Sons of Wilkinson guard—the one whose corpse you've seen." Rogers risked a side-glance, to confirm that Grey was absolutely expressionless. "On the way, we got a chance to talk to that guard. We convinced him that their scheme was madness and that those who participated in it were doomed. We also assured him that it wasn't too late to save himself by throwing in with us. He agreed to take over the ship and bring us here, but in the event he and R'Ghal were both killed."

"Hmm . . . I must say, it's remarkable that you two were able to make this guard see the error of his ways. You must have been extraordinarily persuasive."

Rogers said nothing and concentrated on looking modest, while Grey looked demure. He was only too well aware that their half-true story would have instantly aroused the skepticism of a trained criminal investigator. Fortunately Captain Viglione, however intelligent, was not such an investigator.

Sooner or later, of course, he was going to have some explaining to do for having falsified a report so as to conceal Grey Goldson's Sons of Arnold activities, including her double role in NAISA. But he was confident he would be able to make a case for the importance, at this stage, of continuing to retain her trust.

The explanation he really dreaded eventually making was not to his superiors but to her.

For the present, though, they all had other things on their minds.

"Well, at any rate," said Viglione in a subject-closing tone, "however you managed it, the point is you're here now. And it's a good thing you are, considering the information you've brought—particularly in regard to this joint scheme of theirs to use *Mayflower II* as a weapon against this station." He gave a rueful headshake, as though wondering why they had never thought of the giant colony ship's potential for destruction. "But I gather you didn't learn when they plan to put it into action."

"No, sir, and in fact my impression is that there is no set time. They're holding themselves in readiness, waiting to hear the result of their other operation: seizing a Defiant-class second-rater and turning it over to the Caliphate."

"And," Grey added, "remember what Ethan—that is, Stark—said: They're going to go ahead whether that operation is successful or not. It's probably intended in part as a distraction, to get the Navy's attention fixated far away from Tau Ceti."

Viglione didn't notice her slight slip, as he frowned with concentration and worry. The Defiant class, in addition to being among the largest space warships in existence, were also the most advanced, mounting weapon systems and instrumentation a generation ahead of the chronically laggard Caliphate. For the Caliphate to obtain such a ship intact would be a calamity. "And you don't know when that's due to take place?"

"No . . . or where."

"Well, there are only so many Defiants. Let's see where they are." Viglione glanced at Grey and hesitated momentarily, but apparently decided that under the circumstances security restrictions could be bent. He turned to his computer and began bringing up current orders of battle and deployment schedules. Rogers ran his eye down the list of Defiants and pointed.

"That one. It's got to be."

Viglione nodded slowly. "HMSS *Resolute.* She's en route to Lambda Aurigae—should be almost there, in fact—to show the flag and provide Marine support for our colonists on the fourth planet, New Kashmir. They've had trouble with a Caliphate enclave there, and recently there's been a buildup of Caliphate naval units in the system. So, unlike any of the other Defiants, she's going someplace where there are Caliphate types present to take possession— presumably after she's been seized by traitors among the crew." His expression eloquently expressed his feelings about the last part.

"We've got to get word to the Admiralty on Earth," said Rogers.

"I'll do better than that. In addition to sending one fast courier boat to Earth, I'll send another directly to Lambda Aurigae with a personal message to Ilderim Sharif—he's *Resolute*'s skipper—to be on the alert."

"Unfortunately, Lambda Aurigae is a long way from here."

Viglione gave a nod of glum accord. He fiddled with the computer for a moment. "Forty-seven point thirteen light-years, to be exact. Courier boats are built for speed and little else, but it will still take one...oh, a little more than five and a half standard days to get there. If *Resolute* is on schedule—and knowing Ilderim, she will be—she'll have already been in the Lambda Aurigae system for at least four days."

"So the warning may very well not be in time," said Grey sadly.

"Perhaps not. But the good news is this. You said they're not going to make their move in this system until they get word of the outcome, one way or the other, at Lambda Aurigae. They can't possibly get that word any faster than us, and probably not as fast. So even if they make their attempt on *Resolute* soon after her arrival and dispatch the news immediately, that means we should have six and a half or seven days, starting now, to deal with the threat here, which is *Mayflower II*." Viglione's face grew stern and hard. "I propose to do so without delay."

"What about the Gharnakh station here in this system?" asked Rogers.

"That's secondary, and can be left until later. As you tell the story, that station doesn't threaten us directly, but only through *Mayflower II*. So *that* will be our first priority." Viglione grew brisk. "The Admiralty has always considered the maintenance of any kind of major combat capability here to be neither necessary nor, perhaps, politically desirable. The heaviest ship I've got is HMSS *Rooke*, a fifth-rater, but she will be more than sufficient. Even if they use the Bernheim Drive the Gharnakh'sha have installed on *Mayflower II* and try and get away, *Rooke* is much faster and more maneuverable. She can destroy *Mayflower II*'s pion rocket—it's at the aft end of the ship, far away from everything else—and then demand the surrender of the Sons of Wilkinson and Caliphate people—and Gharnakh'sha, if any—who are aboard."

"You realize, sir, that we're dealing with fanatics," cautioned Rogers.

"I am not unaware of that. If they refuse to surrender, we will reduce that ship to space junk."

Grey drew herself up and spoke formally. "Captain Viglione, as the sole representative of the New American planetary government present, I strongly advise against this course of action. Very strongly."

"Oh? On what grounds, Agent Goldson?"

"Captain, you're not a native of New America. To you, that ship is just that: a ship. An archaic, hopelessly obsolete ship at that. You cannot possibly know—or *feel*—what *Mayflower II* means to New Americans. To us, it is...I hardly know how to put it into words. It's almost like an aged relic—the physical embodiment of our society's foundation myth. If an Imperial warship blasts away at it, even if the physical damage is limited to the destruction of the pion rocket, it will seem like a kind of sacrilege. Resentment would be too weak a word for the public reaction."

"Surely your people would be able to see the necessity of preventing their 'sacred relic' from being used as a weapon of mass murder by terrorists!"

"But you'd be striking *before* they commit an overt act. No subsequent explanations would erase that first impression. I can't imagine anything that would outrage New Americans more."

"Commander Rogers, what is your view?"

"I concur, Captain. It would be a gold mine of propaganda for the Sons of Arnold."

"If we wait until *after* they've committed their 'overt act,' it will be too late!" Viglione shook his head. "What are you proposing? That we sit around and do nothing?"

"Of course not, sir. On our way here, we discussed an alternative plan." *After we had worked out the story of our adventures*, Rogers mentally added. *And, like that story, the rationale for the plan we present to you is going to have to be slightly different from the strict truth.*

"Well, let's hear it."

"Instead of a direct attack on *Mayflower II*, we suggest a covert raid—a 'Trojan horse' operation—that would do no visible damage to the ship and, in fact, could probably be kept from public knowledge."

"But how would you persuade them to let your 'Trojan horse' aboard the ship?"

Let the half-truths begin, thought Rogers. *Or, rather, resume.*

"Agent Goldson is a New American, and is known to the Sons of Arnold thanks to her NAISA investigations. She and I and a squad of Marines could take the civilian ship we came here in to *Mayflower II*. There, Agent Goldson could tell the Sons of Wilkinson people that in the course of her NAISA investigation she's uncovered the existence of their faction—and that she has become a convert to their cause."

"But what about you?"

"The Sons of Arnold were trying to turn me while I was their captive. Our story will be that they succeeded beyond their wildest dreams: now that I know of the Sons of Wilkinson. I've really seen the light. You know—the enthusiasm of the neophyte."

"Do you really think they'd fall for this?"

"Well, sir, the temptation of having one of their own embedded in NAISA, and another in Naval Intelligence, would be awfully hard to resist."

In reality, of course, this plan is based on the fact that they know her to already be a member of the Sons of Arnold. It will just be a matter of convincing them that she's learned of the Sons of Wilkinson faction and wants to join it. So, Rogers told himself, it actually makes better sense than it must seem to Viglione.

Just one problem. We're relying on Stark's statement that he was going directly back to New America, not to Mayflower II, and therefore won't be aboard her. We're further assuming that he didn't bother to tell his people aboard the ship about Grey—in fact, it may have been a sore subject for him—and therefore as far as they know she's simply a Sons of Arnold member in good standing, still further assuming that at least that some of them will know about her in spite of their cell system. Everything rests on that admittedly risky chain of assumptions.

Captain Viglione's lean face wore an expression Rogers imagined was foreign to it: one of agonized indecision. He ran a hand through his short iron-gray hair. "I don't much care for this plan. But your arguments against an open assault are persuasive—and I'm under standing orders to give due weight to the views of the New American government and the sensibilities of the populace. I don't believe I can unilaterally take the responsibility for this decision. Fortunately, I don't have to. The courier boat I send to Earth will carry a request for orders from the Admiralty. The time lag for news from Lambda Aurigae should allow the boat to get there and back before we have to act one way or the other."

"In the meantime, sir," said Rogers, "it's important that we not alert either the New American government or the resident commissioner. Any action they took on New America would tell the Sons of Wilkinson that we know about them and their plan;

it might stampede them into moving up their schedule and going ahead without waiting for word from Lambda Aurigae." The same reasoning, he recalled, had persuaded Grey that the Sons of Arnold leadership could not be informed about the Sons of Wilkinson just yet.

"Hmm . . . It's arguably somewhat irregular for me to withhold this information from Resident Commissioner Tewari. But I see your point. Very well: agreed." Viglione's face cleared and he sat up straighter. "You two will remain aboard this station and work with my staff to hammer out the details of your plan, just in case the Admiralty decides in favor of it." He permitted himself a brief smile. "Stranger things have been known to happen."

CHAPTER SIXTEEN

THE TRANSPARENT IMAGE OF *MAYFLOWER II* FLOATED IN MIDAIR above the table and under the ceiling-mounted holographic projector. Lieutenant Commander Alexander McReynolds of Washington Station's engineering department manipulated the controls, and the ghostly hologram rotated so as to give views from all angles.

"The Gharnakh'sha must not have had any trouble finding room to install a Bernheim Drive," he told his three listeners. "As you can see from this archival image, that ship had a *lot* of space in the stationary hub just aft of the spin habitats, which it used for storage of things which didn't require the sensation of weight: equipment, supplies, prefabricated buildings, everything they thought they'd need to set up a colony. Now, of course, there's none of that aboard—just cavernous empty space."

"Still," said Grey with a skeptical frown, "wouldn't a Bernheim Drive generator for a ship this massive have to be enormous?"

"Not really, as these things go. Stark told you it could only manage a translight pseudovelocity of less than a hundred times lightspeed, right, Commander?" Rogers nodded. "Now, even though this ship naturally wasn't designed with a hull configuration optimized for superior warp-field geometry, that translates to a sublight capability of about ten gees of thrust." All of the engineer's listeners blinked; this was trivial compared to the hundreds of gees produced by Bernheim Drive installations in ordinary use. "So the hyperdense drive coils, which normally make up the great bulk of a Bernheim Drive's mass and volume, don't amount to all that much. Even rounding everything up to reflect what you've told me about the somewhat unsophisticated quality of Gharnakh engineering, I've calculated that a drive with these performance parameters would easily fit into that central hub."

"So you're convinced that's where it is?" demanded Grey.

"I'm certain of it. There's no other really good place for it. And if my calculations are correct, there's also room in that hub for personnel quarters."

"There and not in the spin habitats?"

"Again, I'd wager on it. Commander Rogers, you mentioned that you saw *Mayflower II* when you rendezvoused with Stark's ship. Were the spin habitats rotating or stationary?"

"Stationary, now that you mention it."

"Just as I surmised." McReynolds overflowed with an engineer's self-satisfaction. "It would seem pretty peculiar for them to be rotating when nobody's supposed to be aboard the ship, wouldn't it? No, I imagine that at the same time the Gharnakh'sha installed the Bernheim Drive they also cobbled together some basic, short-term living quarters, with artificial gravity generators to avoid the medical ill effects of extended weightlessness. Those aren't hard to incorporate for a limited volume, you know."

"So," said Rogers thoughtfully, "everything we're after will be in that central hub."

"Conveniently accessible, since that's where the entry port is," Grey added.

"But unfortunately we can't know the details of the interior layout, now that the Gharnakh'sha are finished modifying it." Rogers looked at McReynolds, who gave a nod of acknowledgment.

"That's true. I've prepared some theoretical models of possible deck plans, based on my estimate of the Bernheim Drive's size and shape. But you must understand that these are mere educated guesses."

"What kind of opposition are we going to be facing, Commander?" asked First Lieutenant Yakov Katz of the Royal Space Marines.

Rogers studied the young but hard-faced officer who had been assigned to lead the assault team in the event the plan was approved. The Marines, like the Navy, were an integrated Empire-wide service. Katz was from the Dominion of Israel, whose people were overrepresented in the Empire's combat branches. It was easy to understand why, given its history. The dominion, from its inception, had to face the implacable hostility of its neighbors. For a while, after 1970, there had been a respite as the Caliphate, in its earlier, saner period, had imposed a kind of order on the chaos it had inherited from the old Turkish Empire. But in the 2020s, the Caliphate—vulnerable like all Islamic societies to the siren song of jihad—had fallen permanently under the control of blood-mad fundamentalist fanatics. Ever since, Katz's people had endured chronic terrorism, clandestinely supported by the Caliphate and aiming for the highest possible pitch of obscene horror. They had learned to fight back with grim ruthlessness.

"We don't know," Rogers replied. "Stark said nothing about numbers. He also said nothing, one way or the other, about any Gharnakh'sha being present. He mentioned that, in addition to Sons of Wilkinson members, there are some Caliphate technicians."

"Ah," said Katz with a nod. His eyes were unreadable, but Rogers fancied that he could glimpse behind them the memory of tortured captives, genitally mutilated women and murdered children, which were Caliphate specialties.

"Our advantage will be surprise," Rogers continued. "These people have no reason to expect to have to repel boarders. It's possible that they're not even armed, although of course we're not counting on that. And I certainly wouldn't think they'd be wearing any kind of body armor."

"When they see what's happening," said Grey hopefully, "maybe they'll surrender without a fight."

"I doubt that, ma'am, in light of my experience with fanatics," said Katz. "They tend to fight to the death." Rogers suspected that, at least as far as the Caliphate types were concerned, the wish was father to the thought.

"You're probably right," he said. "Nevertheless, Lieutenant, any surrender offers *will* be accepted. It would be useful to have some prisoners to interrogate."

"Understood, sir."

"And now, Alex, let's see those theoretical deck plans of yours, so we can come up with some alternative tactical scenarios."

❖   ❖   ❖

For the next few cycles of watches that served for "days" aboard Washington Station, they ran practice exercises and shook the assault team down into a smoothly functioning unit. The Rover was too small to carry a full squad and its equipment in addition to Rogers, Grey and McReynolds, so the team would consist of Katz and five handpicked enlisted Marines. Even for them, it would be a tight fit. Indeed, they would have been more than the boat could have accommodated, save for the fact that the Marines' trademark bulky powered combat armor was unnecessary and, in fact, impractical. Likewise, they did not expect to need—or have room to use—any heavy squad-support weaponry like shoulder-fired missile launchers and man-portable plasma guns. (The latter, in any event, could only be used when wearing powered armor or something with equivalent protective value.)

Thus they would travel light, armed with Mark VII Gauss needle carbines, safe weapons for combat inside a space vehicle, against whose bulkheads their sliverlike flechettes would shatter. By the same token, they were largely useless against rigid armor. But they could shred the kind of unarmored personnel the team expected to encounter aboard *Mayflower II*. The Marines were also armed with their standard combat knives, except for Private Narayan Gurung, who carried the vicious forward-curving *kukri* blade of his Gurkha ancestors; it never occurred to anyone to suggest that he not do so. Finally, they each had a bandolier of golf-ball-sized sonic stun grenades. Rogers would carry the Webley Gauss pistol with which he was comfortable. So would Grey, who also demonstrated a familiarity with the weapon that helped reconcile the Marines to her presence in the team. McReynolds would carry a satchel containing assorted special equipment.

In place of the superfluous powered armor, they would wear the flexible "light infantry field suit," whose tough, self-repairing nanofabric material provided a degree of protection which was enhanced by ceramic/metal inserts—rigid plates fitted into torso pockets. The suit could "breathe" through micropores for comfort or, in the presence of hostile conditions, automatically seal itself into a fully insulated multi-environment survival suit, complete with thermocouples woven into the fabric for heating or cooling. It had a very compact back-mounted life-support pack that enabled it, with a clear nanoplastic hood pulled over and fastened, to function as a short-term vacuum suit. The last feature was a source of comfort for those engaged in combat aboard any kind of space habitat, although in the present instance they did not expect to find themselves doing any extravehicular high jinks.

Katz had ruled out the use of combat helmets, with their sophisticated array of holographic HUD, sensor visor, and so forth. It seemed excessive for a mission in cramped quarters. But he had decreed multi-view goggles, whose infrared and light-gathering features might come in handy if—whether by accident or design—the interior lighting failed.

While they planned and practiced, technicians installed a deep-scanner aboard the Rover. It was arguably the most important piece of equipment they had, for it would enable them to determine which—if any—of McReynolds' projected deck plans corresponded with reality. It took X-ray holograms of the interior of an object, and its dedicated computer could "peel away" layers, producing a three-dimensional model. Unfortunately, it took its time about it, and was very short-range. They would have to perform the scan during the last phase of their approach to *Mayflower II*, and hope that phase lasted long enough to complete it.

Time crawled by . . . and Rogers' nerves also began to crawl. Captain Viglione had dispatched his courier boat to Sol promptly, and between there and Tau Ceti was a three-standard-day round trip for such boats. That should allow more than enough time for the Admiralty's orders to reach them well before news from Lambda Aurigae could arrive. But then the third day came and went. So did another day, and another.

We can propel our ships faster than light, thought Rogers, mentally gritting his teeth, *but nobody has ever discovered a way to speed up bureaucratic decision-making.*

So all they could do was wait, while their leeway of six and a half to seven days shrank and shrank.

Rogers was asleep, and in the midst of a troubled dream, when the communicator implanted in his skull sounded off in its obnoxious emergency mode. He made the requisite jaw movement to accept. "Commander Rogers, report to Captain Viglione's office immediately," said a robotic voice. He was out of the bunk instantly, shaking sleep out of his head and scrambling into uniform. Emerging into the passageway, he almost collided with a disheveled Grey Goldson, heading in the same direction.

Lieutenant Katz was already in Viglione's office, looking offensively crisp and wide-awake. McReynolds arrived a couple of seconds after they did. The captain waved them to chairs and began without preamble.

"I have just received word, through the courier service, that the attempt on *Resolute* was made." He raised a hand to cut off any questions. "It failed."

Rogers recalled the present date and time, and did a quick mental calculation. "The ship must have just barely arrived at Lambda Aurigae when they made their move—before your warning reached *Resolute*'s captain."

"Yes. Nevertheless, as the dispatch makes clear, some quick thinking—not to mention boldness—on the part of the ship's helmsman prevented the attempt from succeeding. *Resolute* is still in our hands."

"Thank God for that!" breathed Rogers.

"No argument there. Nevertheless, this brings matters to a head in this system. Their people aboard *Mayflower II* are awaiting this news."

"And," Grey reminded him, "they intend to go ahead with their plan whether the news is of success or of failure."

Viglione's dark eyes were somber indeed. "As I said, I received this message via the Navy courier service. It was sent out to all commands on a top priority basis. In other words, it got here as fast as is humanly possible with present-day technology. Now, regardless of what means the Caliphate or the Sons of Wilkinson had prepared in the Lambda Aurigae system to get the word to Tau Ceti, their people here cannot possibly have received it yet—which, of course, is why *Mayflower II* is still in its orbit. But we have no way of knowing how much time we have until they do. We cannot afford to assume that it will be very long."

"And the Admiralty is still dithering," said Rogers harshly. "Captain, we can no longer wait for the red tape on Earth to unwind." He did not add *You have to make the decision on your own, one way or another*, partly because he had no business saying that to a superior officer, but mostly because it went without saying.

"No, we can't. It's now or never." Viglione buried his face in his hands, and none of them felt inclined to disturb the man on whom this weight of responsibility had suddenly descended. But the silence lasted only a few moments. The captain raised his head, and his expression held nothing but calm resolve. "I still don't like this scheme of yours. But I'm going to let you try it. After you leave, without being conspicuous about it, I'll deploy *Rooke* and my lighter ships in a screen, to try and deal with *Mayflower II* in case you fail."' He gave Grey a stern look. "At that stage, I will *not* let this station be destroyed if I can help it, regardless of New American sensibilities."

"I understand, Captain," Grey assured him.

"Very well, then. Lieutenant Katz, how soon can your men be ready to go?"

"Marines are always ready to go, sir." From some, it would have been braggadocio. From Katz, it was a simple statement of fact.

"Just one thing, Captain," said Rogers. "As you've pointed out, time is of the essence. And under slower-than-light pseudo-acceleration, it's going to take a certain amount of time to cross fourteen astronomical units. I suggest we take a leaf from their book and do a faster-than-light hop."

Viglione looked at him sharply. "I realize you're a qualified pilot, Commander, but do you feel up to this?"

"I believe so, sir."

"But Robert," Grey protested, "you said it yourself: *Mayflower II* is inside Tau Ceti's Secondary Limit."

"Oh, don't worry; I have no intention of wrecking the Rover's Bernheim Drive. I plan to hop to a point just outside the Secondary Limit, then proceed the rest of the way in slower-than-light mode."

"Won't they be suspicious, if a ship kills its warp field that close to them?" wondered McReynolds. "Of course," he instantly answered his own question, "they'll probably not notice; they'll have no reason to be looking for it. But then, when we approach them seemingly out of nowhere..."

"This particular Rover is fitted with a sophisticated stealth suite—as they know, since it was the Sons of Arnold that installed it. We'll approach under that, then disengage it. Grey, as part of her story about wanting to join them, can say she stole it, and has a pilot who's also seen the light."

"Well," said Viglione gruffly, "I suppose this can't make your plan much more harebrained than it already is." It seemed he wanted to say something else but then thought better of it. "All right. Get going—and good luck."

CHAPTER SEVENTEEN

AT ITS MAXIMUM TRANSLIGHT PSEUDOVELOCITY, THE ROVER TOOK precisely 3.669 seconds to cover fourteen astronomical units. To its occupants, the stars seemed to rush colorfully astern and then, after a mere instant of mind-numbing void, flow back with equal rapidity before settling back into the pattern of the constellations as viewed from Tau Ceti.

Rogers rather smugly noted that they had arrived at almost precisely the point he had calculated, just outside the Secondary Limit, in a volume of space which the occupants of *Mayflower II* would have no particular reason to be observing. And they had arrived with the stealth suite fully activated. Now he shaped a slower-than-light course for the great old colony ship. With the course set in and the autopilot on duty, he exchanged a look with Grey, who sat beside him on the control bridge. Then he stood up and descended to the main cabin, where McReynolds and the Marines waited.

"Lieutenant," he told Katz, "we'll shortly be going out of stealth, and Agent Goldson will establish communication with *Mayflower II*. It is, of course, essential that none of you get caught in the video pickup—it would give the game away. Therefore, you'll have to wait in the cargo compartment aft until she's through conversing with them." He smiled. "You'll be like sardines in there, but it won't be for long."

"Right, Commander. Sergeant O'Malley, let's go."

"Aye aye, sir. Come on, you men."

Rogers turned to McReynolds. "Same goes for you, Alex, and for the same reason. Afterwards, you can come out and operate the deep-scanner." It was one of the engineer's two functions, the other being the deactivation of the Gharnakh Bernheim Drive the moment they had secured it, for they had no way of knowing how close the Sons of Wilkinson were to being able to initiate their plan. He nodded and followed the Marines.

Rogers rejoined Grey on the bridge. They shared a knowing look. The explanation he had just given for clearing the cabin had been perfectly true, as far as it went. But there was an additional reason. Grey's spiel was not going to be what everyone from Captain Viglione on down had been led to believe. Among other things, it would reveal her Sons of Arnold membership. No one else aboard the Rover could be allowed to overhear it.

Of course, if any of the Sons of Wilkinson were taken alive and talked, things could become awkward. *I'll just have to cross that bridge when I come to it*, Rogers philosophized, demonstrating that his originality had limits.

It didn't take long to come within a range where even the most perfunctory radar surveillance would surely detect them, and decelerate to zero pseudovelocity. Only then did Rogers deactivate the stealth suite. Simultaneously, Grey hailed *Mayflower II*. There was no reply—unsurprisingly, as the great ship was supposed to be empty.

"I said this is Grey Goldson," she snapped. "Whoever is listening, you probably don't know me." Rogers remembered the Sons of Arnold's cell system. "But ask around—there'll be somebody who recognizes the name."

A few seconds passed. Then the comm screen awoke to life, and a face was staring out of it, with a couple of others crowding in behind him. "Grey? It *is* you! But...but...how did you know—?"

"Yes, it is me, Gavin. And yes, I know about the Sons of Wilkinson. I also know what you're doing aboard that ship. And I'm with you!"

Gavin's eyes grew even wider. "But how did you find out about us? The last we heard, you had just captured that Naval Intelligence officer who had arrived on New America."

Rogers commanded himself not to let his relief show. *So we were right. Stark didn't tell his people aboard* Mayflower II *about Grey. They're badly out of date about what Grey has been up to.*

"I knew about you before that," Grey was saying, "through my work at NAISA. But I suppressed it. More than that, I planted false scents to lead NAISA investigators in wrong directions—it's thanks to me that you haven't been found out. You see, the more I found out, the more I knew you were right. I realized Dr. Bricknell and the others are living in a dream world. We need new leadership. I was ready to approach Ethan—yes, I know he's the leader—but he had left New America to come here. So I stole this boat, with the special stealth suite we put in—that's how I got away in it—to follow him. Is he still here?" she asked with every appearance of innocence. It all had just enough internal logic to hold together if one didn't examine it too closely. Gavin didn't seem inclined to do so, in his present still-somewhat-flustered mental state.

"No, Ethan's gone back planetside. But who's with you? Somebody must be piloting the boat."

"Yes, and that's the best part! Remember the Naval Intelligence officer we were holding—Robert Rogers is his name. As you may be aware, Dr. Bricknell and the others were trying to persuade him of the justice of the Sons of Arnolds' cause—he's North American by birth, remember. Well, they succeeded beyond their wildest dreams! He became such an enthusiastic convert that I covertly told him about the Sons of Wilkinson. He saw at once that you were right about the need for direct action." Grey assumed a slightly shamefaced look. "I'd learned that Ethan planned to turn him over to the Caliphate people, so I spirited him away before that could be done. I felt like I was deceiving Ethan, who didn't even know—and still doesn't—that I even know about the Sons of Wilkinson. But it had to be done, because Rogers is too valuable to us to be thrown to the wolves."

Rogers watched the face in the comm screen intently. This added another whole level of implausibility to the story, and Gavin's skepticism was palpable.

"Grey, how sure of him are you? How can you be certain this isn't a trick?"

"Believe me, Gavin, I'll vouch for him. He wants in . . . but clandestinely, so he can work for us inside Naval Intelligence."

"My God!" Gavin's doubts were visibly washed away by sheer avidity. "What a coup! And I'm sure I don't need to tell you how glad

I am that you're with us. Come ahead and dock here. Fasten to the personnel airlock of the central hub. Do you know where that is?"

"Yes, I looked up the ship's plans."

"Good. The exterior is unchanged, so you shouldn't have any trouble. I'm looking forward to meeting this Rogers. What an ironic name!" Gavin turned to one of the men behind him. "Jack, go tell Cranston to come to the entry port whenever he's finished what he's doing with the drive. But don't tell him why—I want to surprise him. Signing off for now, Grey."

"Signing off." She cut the connection, and at once slumped into her chair. The animated expression she had shown Gavin abruptly drained from her face, leaving a sick look. Rogers was fairly sure he knew why.

"These people are friends of mine," she said, not looking at him. "Yes, I know, they've gone rogue and have to be stopped. But it's very hard, lying to them...much less—"

"I've given orders that they're to be spared if they surrender," he reminded her. "But yes, I know it's hard. And you did well." He gave her shoulder a reassuring squeeze, then set in the course, using the lowest thrust he could without arousing suspicion, for he wanted to give McReynolds time for his scan. Then he hopped down to the cabin and went aft to the cargo compartment. The light infantry field suits, with their multi-environmental features, helped suppress the tension-sweat of overcrowded bodies.

"All right, they bought it. Lieutenant, you and your men come on out into the cabin and hold yourselves in readiness. Alex, we'll be in deep-scanner range shortly."

The old colony ship was soon a naked-eye object, such was her size. Rogers maneuvered toward a rendezvous with her, more slowly than he needed to but not unreasonably so. To the opposite side of him from Grey, McReynolds sat at his jury-rigged control board and activated it. There was such a thing as a deep-scan detector that could warn the subjects of such a scan that it was being performed, but Rogers was confident that there was no such detector aboard *Mayflower II*; it was an expensive piece of equipment, and the Sons of Wilkinson would have no reason to think they'd need it.

As McReynolds manipulated his controls with great delicacy, Rogers risked an occasional side-glance at the small holo-cube where a ghostly three-dimensional image of the central hub's interior was forming in the slow, onion-peel way of the deep-scanner.

But most of his attention was, of necessity, focused on the view-forward, in which *Mayflower II* was inexorably growing.

"How much longer, Alex?" he asked in a tight voice.

"I need more time. I still don't have enough to determine which of the theoretical layouts is the correct one." McReynolds didn't even consider the possibility that none of them were. He had worked out all the deck plans he considered practical, given the irreducible parameters of the Bernheim Drive, and assigned numbers to them for convenience. Rogers and Katz had worked out a prepared tactical plan for each of them, and the Marines had memorized all of those plans. As soon as they knew which one to follow, they would know just what to do, unhesitatingly.

"I'll take as long as I can." Rogers deliberately fumbled his approach, necessitating a course adjustment, which he made in a wobbly way, then lined up for a second try. The Bernheim Drive didn't repeal the laws of motion, but it made possible—albeit with difficulty—a kind of blundering that would have been out of the question in space with rockets. He didn't care if those observing him were laughing at him as a clumsy pilot. But he mustn't seem like a totally incompetent one; that wouldn't ring true.

He was wondering how much more buffoonery he could get away with when McReynolds finally called out, "Got it! It's similar, though not identical, to number three."

Katz, who had crowded onto the tiny bridge, looked over the engineer's shoulder and nodded. "Yes... not quite the same kind of access to the berthing spaces, but otherwise close enough. Sergeant O'Malley," he called out, "it's layout number three. Stand by."

"Aye aye, sir."

Mayflower II grew and grew in the viewscreen, and as they drew close enough to make out details her enormous size came into focus. Of course, the detail in which they were primarily interested was the airlock. In one respect, the New Americans' desire to preserve the ship in her pristine state had yielded to practicality. Originally, there had been two airlocks, connected to the nose sections of the two orbit-to-ground shuttles—huge spaceplanes docked in cradles just aft of the central hub. These had been replaced, one with a large cargo lock and one with a much smaller one for personnel. Both were standardized in this day and age; even a craft as small as a Rover like theirs could adapt its airlock to the personnel lock and seal to it.

With no further reason to delay, but avoiding a suspiciously sudden, dramatic improvement in piloting skills, Rogers maneuvered his diminutive craft until the two airlocks were aligned. Then, using the Rover's very low-capacity tractor beam to finalize contact, he initiated the magnetic anchoring process, followed by gas-tight sealing. He met Grey's eyes. "Ready?"

"Ready," she said, and he heard nothing but steadiness. They stood up and went to the airlock while the Marines held back out of the line of sight of anyone at the other end of the linked airlocks.

The plan was essentially simple. Rogers and Grey, dressed in nondescript civilian clothing over vests of nanoplastic ballistic armor and carrying Webleys tucked under their belts at the small of the back, would enter *Mayflower II* and use the threat (hopefully all that would be required) of their needlers to secure that end of the airlock. Then the Marines would storm through and proceed through passageways concerning whose layout they now had a fair idea, suppressing all opposition and taking control of the Bernheim Drive. *It ought to work*, Rogers assured himself, *given the element of total surprise.*

They stepped through into the relatively cavernous spaces of the arklike old ship. Gavin was there, as were two other men. As Rogers more than half expected, they were unarmed, aboard this ship where they were among no one but friends. Gavin stepped forward, smiling broadly.

"Grey! And this must be Commander Rogers. It's a pleasure to see you. And there's someone I want you to meet...ah!" He added, as two figures appeared, ascending a lift tube behind him and to his left. "Here's Cranston now."

One of the two was the man Gavin had previously addressed as "Jack." As the other, presumably Cranston, emerged from the lift tube, Rogers felt an oddly ominous sense of recognition, although he couldn't place the man. Then, as he was trying to recall where he had seen that face, Cranston's mouth fell open and his eyes bulged.

Rogers stared too—for now he remembered. This man had been one of the guards who had flanked him and Grey aboard Ethan Stark's vessel. *So*, he thought in an instant of suspended time, *before returning to New America, Stark sent Cranston over here to this ship, after he had witnessed the whole scene and therefore knew about Grey's current status—*

Then Cranston's shout shattered his thoughts. "Grab them! It's a trick!"

CHAPTER EIGHTEEN

FOR SOME TINY FRACTION OF A SECOND, THE TABLEAU HELD. Then it shattered into an explosion of action.

Gavin, with a snarl, lunged for Rogers. They grappled before Rogers could reach behind him for his needler. Even as he struggled, Rogers saw out of the corner of his right eye that Cranston, followed by Jack, had sprung for Grey. But a man to Gavin's left, still in a state of stunned immobility, got in his way. This gave Grey time to bring her Webley around and fire it on autoburst setting. Cranston's face seemed to fly apart in a shower of blood and shredded flesh, muscle and bone. But then Jack and Gavin's left-hand man were on top of her, the latter tackling her around the knees while Jack gripped the wrist of her gun-arm and wrenched the Webley out of her hand.

It was only with a small fraction of his consciousness that Rogers saw all this. For the most part, he concentrated on breaking free of Gavin's grip with a judo move, followed by a short jab to the solar plexus. Gavin collapsed with a shrieking gasp. But at appreciably the same instant, before Rogers could recover, the man who had been standing to Gavin's right grasped him around the neck and forced him down onto his knees, applying a choke hold. With his face almost shoved into the man's midriff, Rogers struggled to breathe. But then he glimpsed a quick movement from behind him, and a sudden flask of steel. The man holding him screamed and released him, using both hands to clutch his blood-gushing midriff to hold his guts in. Then Private Gurung's *kukri* slashed him across the throat. The Gurkha grinned at Rogers as the other Marines crowded past him.

Katz must have heard the noise at this end and ordered his men through without waiting for our signal, thought Rogers as he staggered to his feet and pulled out his Webley. Even as he did so, the Marines put a fusillade of flechettes through the man grasping Grey's legs. But Jack got behind her and, seizing her around the upper arms and using her as a shield, held her Webley to the side of her head.

"Don't move or this traitorous bitch dies!" he rasped.

Everyone momentarily froze, for despite Grey's struggles neither Rogers nor any of the Marines could risk a shot. Jack drew a deep breath and broke the silence by roaring at the top of his lungs, *"Alert! We're under attack! Go to—"*

Before he could say anything else, Grey abruptly stopped struggling. She went limp and sagged in his arm, her knees folding under her. The unexpected move momentarily put him off balance; his grasp weakened and the needler wavered. Then, with a sudden lurch, she broke free, twisted around and, with frantic strength, took hold of his wrist and forced the needler up. He got off a shot that practically clipped her hair; the steel needle shattered against a bulkhead. But her sideways move had exposed him. Before anyone else could react, Katz squeezed off an autoburst that he held precisely on target. Jack's chest was ripped open, and his heart exploded out his back in a fountain of blood. Already dead, he collapsed atop Grey. Rogers ran to her and helped her out from under the corpse and up to her feet. Her face was a mask of self-control as she looked around at the carnage.

"All right, Lieutenant," Rogers rapped. "I don't know if any of the others heard him, but we need to get moving. Leave one man to guard him." He pointed at Gavin, who was still gasping on the deck in fetal position. "Otherwise, let's go with the plan."

"Aye aye, sir." They had agreed beforehand on the need to secure their rear and the point of contact with their own vessel before advancing further into the bowels of *Mayflower II*. "Campbell, take charge of this prisoner and keep an eye on the lift for anybody coming down from the upper decks. Adams, Johnson, cover the two branching passageways and shoot anything that comes down them—especially that one. It leads to the living quarters, right, sir?"

"Right," affirmed McReynolds, who had followed the Marines through the linked airlocks.

"Agent Goldson," Katz continued, "perhaps you should remain here and—"

"Not on your life!" Grey snapped. "If I can possibly do anything to minimize any further killing, I'm going to do it."

There was no need for further discussion, for they had all known what they had to do from the moment they knew they were dealing with McReynolds' "number three" deck plan. Rogers, Grey, McReynolds, Katz, Sergeant O'Malley and Private Gurung ran to the "down" lift tube that led to the Bernheim Drive controls two levels below, on the bottom deck. Katz tossed two of his stun grenades into the shaft, at intervals of a few seconds. They waited long enough for the grenades to go off (hopefully after having had enough time to reach bottom), then Rogers led the way into the tube. Like all lift tubes aboard *Mayflower II*, it had been installed by the New Americans in yet another departure from strict historical authenticity, for such things hadn't existed in 2120. It was a heavy-duty version, designed to accommodate cargo as well as personnel, so all six of them could fit in.

They had floated down through one level and were in the second when, with sickening abruptness, the tractor beamlike effect ceased to hold them.

Somebody must have heard Jack's shout and immediately got to work shutting it down, thought Rogers as the background artificial gravity field of one New America gee took hold and they fell the rest of the way. Almost before they had time to be startled, they landed on the deck. Fortunately, they didn't have far to fall. Rogers managed to gather up his knees just before impact, but he cut it too close to pull off a roll, stumbling and falling instead. And having been first into the lift, he was at the bottom of the pile. Grey fell on top of him, which under any other circumstances he might have enjoyed. The others landed in a heap that would have brought tears to the eyes of a parachute instructor.

As they began to get up, a man leaped from behind a nearby corner of a passageway, where he had doubtless been concealed from the effects of the stun grenades. Screaming something in Arabic, he opened fire with a Gauss needle carbine similar to the Mark VII. *So the Caliphate people here, at least, are armed*, thought Rogers. A couple of the tiny flechettes stitched Sergeant O'Malley's upper right arm, but his armor inserts protected his torso. A fusillade of return fire from the Marines practically ripped the man apart. Gurung tossed a stun grenade into the passageway so that it rebounded from the far bulkhead and vanished behind the corner before detonating.

McReynolds knelt beside O'Malley and gave him a pre-prepared single-shot injection from the very minimal first-aid packet in his satchel. It would deaden the pain and slow the bleeding. "Sergeant, stay here," ordered Katz. "Can you cover the branching corridors behind us?"

"I think so, sir," said O'Malley.

"I'll trade you this for your Mark VII, Sergeant," said Rogers, handing him his Webley. "You can use it one-handed."

"Thank you, sir."

"All right," said Katz. "The passageway around that corridor leads to the Bernheim Drive controls. Everybody ready? *Go!*"

They rounded the corner, weapons ready. The passageway was empty save for a Near Eastern-looking man who lay with a needler beside him on the deck, where Gurung's stun grenade had rendered him unconscious. Katz stood over him and, with his Mark VII, put a single flechette through his temple. Grey seemed about to say something, but thought better of it. They trotted the rest of the way to the end of the passageway, where their objective lay behind a closed hatch. Rogers slid his hand over the entry panel, but, to no one's surprise, the hatch did not open.

No orders were necessary. McReynolds reached into his satchel and took out a circular object about the size of a pie plate but two inches thick. He slapped it onto the entry panel, where it clanged home magnetically, then activated a timer on its underside. They all flattened themselves against the bulkheads to the sides of the hatch. After a couple of eternal seconds, the deck jumped under their feet and a deafening crash battered their ears in the enclosed space as the shaped charge blasted through the hatch, leaving it hanging ajar.

Katz sprang out from the bulkhead and kicked the hatch open. He barely had time to jump back and avoid a spray of flechettes that came from within, accompanied by a shout of *"Allahu akbar!"* He and Gurung each lobbed a stun grenade through the hatch, and the firing ceased. They all crowded into the control room, with its banks of controls and readouts and its wide transparency overlooking the drive coils.

There had been two armed Caliphate men. One had been caught by the narrow jet of molten metal blown out by the shaped charge and was very dead. The other, who had been doing the firing, was lying crumpled on the deck, still loosely holding his needler. There were two other unconscious men, both unarmed and both with the look of New Americans. Katz took a step toward the live shooter.

"Prisoners, Lieutenant," Rogers reminded him, quietly but firmly.

"Right, Commander," said Katz after a barely perceptible hesitation. "Private Gurung, let's find something to tie these three up with—the grenades' effect doesn't last."

Rogers and Grey examined the unconscious Sons of Wilkinson. "Anybody you know?" Rogers murmured, too low for Katz to hear.

"No," she replied in kind. "Remember about the cell system."

Katz took out his pocket communicator and set it on "speaker" mode. "Campbell, any action back there?"

"Not much sir. Somebody started to come from the living quarters, but they jumped back after a couple of warning shots. No return fire, or any other further activity."

"They must all be Sons of Wilkinson," said Grey. "Lieutenant, I think I can probably talk them into surrendering—especially," she added emphatically, "If I go in alone, without your men present. Don't worry, I'll go armed."

Katz looked a question at Rogers, who nodded. "Very well. But if they try any funny business, just shout for Campbell and the others. They'll simply stun everybody in there."

As Grey left, McReynolds shoved an unconscious man off the main control panel across which he had collapsed, and seated himself. For several minutes, he fiddled with the controls. Rogers began to fidget, but left the engineer alone.

Finally, McReynolds sat back with a sigh and looked up at Rogers. "All right: done. Sorry it took so long, but this is a Caliphate model I'm unfamiliar with. However, the drive is now deactivated. It would take anyone some time to get it on line again. And now that we have some leisure, I'll go down there"—he gestured through the transparency—"and do a proper job of sabotage."

"Good." Rogers turned to Katz. "Lieutenant, now I think we can let Captain Viglione know he can go ahead and contact the resident commissioner and tell all. There's no further reason not to take action against the Sons of Wilkinson."

Nor, he did not add, *is there any reason for Grey not to tell the Sons of Arnold leadership about their radical splinter group . . . and their new convert Robert Rogers.*

Which means things are apt to get sticky.

CHAPTER NINETEEN

A LASERCOM MESSAGE, LIMITED TO LIGHTSPEED, WOULD HAVE taken very nearly two hours to cover fourteen astronomical units. Therefore they hastily herded their prisoners aboard the Rover, with three Marines including the injured Sergeant O'Malley to guard them, while McReynolds, Lieutenant Katz and the other two Marines remained aboard *Mayflower II*, just in case. Rogers then took them outside Tau Ceti's Secondary Limit, engaged the warp field, and performed another 3.669-second faster-than-light hop to the vicinity of the hollowed-out asteroid that was Washington Station.

O'Malley was transferred to sickbay, and the prisoners to the brig (with Gavin silently glowering his hate at Grey and the Caliphate technician muttering in a tone that made Rogers just as glad he didn't understand Arabic). Minutes later, he and Grey were in the captain's office.

"Well, congratulations," Viglione greeted them, motioning them to chairs. "You may be interested to know that, while you were gone, word finally arrived from the Admiralty." He smiled tightly. "They said your plan was still under consideration by a special committee."

"I hope you don't get into trouble for having given us the go-ahead on your own, Captain," said Grey.

"Under the circumstances, I doubt it. When they sort everything out, the timing of our receipt of the word from Lambda Aurigae will be apparent, and they'll realize we had no choice but to act. I'm sure they'll retroactively approve a successful operation."

And probably try to claim credit for it, Rogers thought sourly. But he was certain Viglione was right. Micromanagement across interstellar distances was impossible. With instantaneous communications left behind on Earth, naval officers on distant stations were as much on their own as they had been in the Age of Sail, and of necessity possessed a latitude for the exercise of individual initiative wider than any had enjoyed since then.

"Needless to say," Viglione continued, "I'll dispatch a courier boat to Sol with a report to the Admiralty on your success. I'll also transmit a lasercom to the resident commissioner, bringing him up to date on everything. Of course, we're thirteen AUs from New America, so it will take more than one and three-quarters hours to get there."

Rogers and Grey exchanged a quick glance. "Captain," said Rogers, "I suggest that time is of the essence. We don't *think* anybody aboard *Mayflower II* sent off a message that they were under attack, but we can't be sure of that. And if they did, it would only take...oh, a little less than eleven and a half minutes to get to New America. So, depending on when it was fired off, the Sons of Wilkinson could receive it very shortly, if they haven't already. And such a message would tell them that we're on to them, so they'd undoubtedly start going as deep underground as they can burrow. Against this eventuality, we need to act against them without delay. If in fact no such message was sent, no harm done."

"What are you proposing, Commander?"

"Let me and Agent Goldson take the Rover we came in and do a five-second translight hop to a point as close as I can get to the Eithinoha/New America system without being inside Tau Ceti's Secondary Limit. From there, it won't take long to reach the planet at maximum sublight pseudo-acceleration, and practically no time for a message from us to reach the resident commissioner and the New American government. Then, even if the Sons of Wilkinson do know, or are about to know, that their plan has been aborted, we'll be able to get started while they're still assimilating the news."

And, thought Rogers, exchanging another brief eye-contact with Grey, *she'll be able to get word to the Sons of Arnold leadership. Or so she thinks.*

"Are you sure you feel up to doing an in-system hop?" asked Viglione. "You've just been through a rather intense experience."

"I'm sure, sir."

"As am I, Captain," said Grey, dashing Rogers' never-very-confident hope that she would spare him what was coming by remaining on Washington Station.

"Very well. In the meantime, I'm going to send *Rooke* and all the sixth-raters I've got toward the Gharnakh station."

"They'll have to go sublight, Captain," said Rogers. "Unlike this station, they're in the plane of the debris disk, where it's at its densest, so it would be unsafe to come out of warp anywhere nearby. Maybe they put it there for that very reason."

"Well, there's no hurry, since that station isn't threatening us directly—or even indirectly, anymore. I gather you weren't able to obtain any detailed information on their defenses."

"No, I just got a brief glimpse of some laser turrets. The station's pretty big, but it doesn't have the look of a purpose-built orbital fortress."

"Hmm...My first dispatch to the Admiralty included a request for reinforcements. Maybe I should wait for them before taking action. For now, I'll have my ships keep an eye on that station."

"And prevent any transfers of personnel from it," suggested Grey. "As far as we know, Khalid al-Malani is still there."

"Ah." Viglione's expression said all that needed to be said. "All right. We'll handle that. You two had better get moving."

"Right, Captain," said Rogers. "But first, could you have your communications officer download to the Rover's brain the same message you've already sent to the resident commissioner? We'll just fire it off as soon as we come out of warp."

"Yes, that's simple enough."

"Thank you, sir. And on the way, I'll attach an addendum to it."

"Right. Dismissed."

"What was that about an 'addendum,' Robert?" asked Grey afterwards as they hurried through the passageways toward the docking bay.

"Oh, just a request to Resident Commissioner Tewari to

expedite our landing clearance and have a security detail meet us at the spaceport." *Which*, he told himself, *is true as far as it goes.* He paused, looking thoughtful. "You know, I don't think you should broadcast a message to Dr. Bricknell and the others from space. The wrong people might hear it."

"That's probably wise," she said reluctantly. "We don't know how deeply, and in what positions, the Sons of Wilkinson have infiltrated the organization."

"Right," he said with a sage nod. "You'd better go and meet with them in person as soon as we land."

"You think so?"

"Definitely. I tell you what: To save time, I'll specifically ask them in my addendum to bring a glide car to the spaceport for you. We'll tell them you need it to go to NAISA headquarters."

"Thanks, Robert," she said with a smile.

He didn't trust himself to reply.

Rogers switched the warp field on and off, and they found themselves close to where he had intended. He immediately set a sunward course that would take them to New America, already visible as part of a planetary doublet.

He turned to Grey. "You look tired. Pretty used up, in fact."

"Yes. I think delayed reaction to...what happened aboard *Mayflower II* is starting to set in."

"We've got a little while," he urged. "Why don't you go down to the cabin and get some rest while I prepare the message?"

"Thanks. I think I will." She stepped down from the bridge and sprawled in a recliner.

Rogers busied himself with editing the message. His additions contained all he had told her...and a good deal more besides. After transmitting it, he slumped in his chair, alone with his inner conflicts.

By the time the Rover went to photon thrusters and slid between Eithinoha and New America on its final approach, Tewari had cleared a path for them through the usual landing formalities. They bypassed the orbital terminal and, under the medium-high sun of one of New America's daylight "days," settled down on grav repulsion to a specially reserved site at Patrick Henry Spaceport, close to the terminal. As they disembarked, the security men from the Residency, in civilian clothes concealing flexible body armor, stepped forth from a row of parked glide cars, innocent of official markings, to meet them.

Patrick Logan led the security detail. Grey gave him a sharp look, but continued to play the game of not knowing what his real job was, even though she did know, and he knew that she knew, and she knew that he knew that she knew.

"Why, Assistant Secretary Logan," she greeted pleasantly, "I wouldn't have expected to see you here, in this sort of capacity."

"The Residency is so understaffed, we all find ourselves doing odd jobs," he replied blandly.

"Did you bring a glide car for Agent Goldson, as I requested?" asked Rogers. "She needs to report in to her superiors at NAISA without delay."

"Certainly, Commander. That one over there."

"Grey," said Rogers, turning to her, "you'd better get moving."

"Right." She smiled at him. He managed to smile back. Then she got into the indicated glide car and was gone, trailing a low hum and the inevitable puffs of disturbed dust.

As soon as she was out of sight, Rogers turned to Logan, his face set and hard. "Did you install the tracking device in that car?"

"Affirmative, Commander, as per your instructions." Logan led the way to his own car and unfolded an inconspicuous segment of the dashboard, revealing a liquid-crystal screen. At the touch of a button the screen came to life as a glowing map, currently centered on their part of the spaceport. A blinking dot of red light moved along the road Grey had just taken, proceeding toward nearby New Philadelphia.

"If I may say so, Commander, you've done a brilliant job of making a tool of her to lead us to the Sons of Arnold headquarters."

"Thank you," Rogers' two words were so gruff as to verge on curtness, and Logan unconsciously came to something resembling a position of attention. "Now, what about NAISA? Did they agree to cooperate with us on this?"

"Yes, sir. Your message didn't give us much time to contact the New American authorities and bring them up to date—in fact, we were still bringing *ourselves* up to date, and I'm not sure we've completely done so yet. There's quite a lot to assimilate, what with all your adventures, especially the existence of these, uh, Gharnakh'sha. But the parts about the Sons of Wilkinson and what they intended to do with *Mayflower II* were clear enough. NAISA will do as you suggested. They've got their people aloft in aircars, waiting for our signal to converge."

"Good. Very good. This has to be a joint operation—it can't be seen as the Empire riding roughshod over local law enforcement. By the way," he added, seemingly as an afterthought, "in your communications with them, did your people do as I requested and conceal the details of just how we're going about pinpointing our objective?"

"Why, yes; we just spoke vaguely about unspecified sources of information. Everything about Grey Goldson's affiliation with the Sons of Arnold was withheld from NAISA and the New American government in general. We were a little puzzled as to why you wanted that done, but—"

"Never mind." Rogers didn't let his relief show. And he decided some kind of explanation might, after all, be in order. "Actually, Captain Viglione on Washington Station doesn't know it yet; I had to keep it from him in her presence, for what I'm sure are obvious reasons. I just wanted to avoid any possibility of some kind of slip down here that would alert her." This was pretty thin, he knew, so he hastened to change the subject. "All right, let's get going. We don't want to look like a parade, so our cars will take separate, parallel routes. This car will be the command car, keeping the others headed in the right direction and also coordinating with the NAISA aircars."

Logan gave instructions to his men, and they began moving out. One of Logan's men drove the command car, which held Rogers and Logan himself, who kept an eye on the scrolling map and gave instructions to the other cars, marked by green dots, as they followed the coastal road south toward New Philadelphia, spaced widely so as to be inconspicuous. Once they entered the city, Logan directed the cars onto alternate streets, all following the blinking red light as it moved away from the waterfront. He also kept in contact with the hovering NAISA aircars.

Rogers studied the map. Grey was headed toward the city's landward outskirts. "I have a feeling," he told Logan, "that she's going to the abandoned warehouse where I was first held prisoner. The leadership probably moved back there after Stark's bogus 'raid' didn't materialize."

"Will you recognize it when you see it?"

"Not really. I never saw it from the city side. But from what I did see, I've got a pretty clear idea of where it is." He indicated an area of the map. "And that's where she's going. Speed up, and tell the other cars to start converging."

They entered a rather run-down district on the city's fringes, and the gap between the blinking red light and their green one began to close. Presently, they could see Grey's car ahead, driving along an otherwise deserted street which, at its end, opened out into a large bare space at the front of a sprawling hulk of an old warehouse.

"That's it!" said Rogers. "It's got to be. Quick, cut her off before she can enter that open area—they're probably watching it."

The driver applied maximum lateral thrust, and the glide car fairly screamed ahead. Catching up with its quarry, it swerved around to the right, then made a hard left as it passed. Rogers caught a glimpse of a startled Grey Goldson, as she jerked her glide car to the left and, making almost a hundred-and-eighty-degree turn, sought to dart down a side street. But at that moment, one of Logan's other cars emerged from that street and turned broadside to her. As she screeched to a halt to avoid a collision, Logan's drive brought their car up against the rear of hers, so she was immobilized.

Two security men emerged from the newly arrived cars, opened the door of the trapped car, and hauled Grey out. Exiting Logan's car, Rogers saw her from the side as she furiously threw off the grip of a man holding her upper arm.

"Get your hands off me! I'm Special Agent Grey Goldson of NAISA. Whoever you are, you have no right—"

Then she saw Rogers, and froze.

CHAPTER TWENTY

ROGERS WALKED AROUND THE GLIDE CAR AND FACED GREY squarely. The light-colored eyes that held his were pure ice.

"We can't let you go in there. Stark knows about you—and the last he knew, you were being taken to the Gharnakh station. If you appear, wanting to talk to Dr. Bricknell and the others, it will just tell him that something has gone wrong."

"But you let me lead you to this headquarters. Maneuvered me into it, in fact."

"It was necessary. As soon as the NAISA people arrive—they're in on this operation too—we'll deal with the Sons of Wilkinson."

"And you'll 'deal with' the Sons of Arnold while you're at it." She shook her head slowly. "So everything you've told me about coming to see our side of the story has been one long lie."

"To repeat, it was necessary."

"You know," she said, almost conversationally, "NAISA keeps confidential dossiers on various key Imperial intelligence operatives. When we got the word that you were coming to New America and I was appointed liaison officer, I looked yours up. It described you as one devious, Machiavellian bastard. I should have paid more attention to it."

"And if you had—what then? The Sons of Wilkinson might well have gotten away with their crazy scheme to destroy Washington

145

Station. And what would that have accomplished? *Not* the glorious uprising they were fantasizing about—you know that as well as I do. You said yourself that it would have just discredited the Sons of Arnold. It would also have caused the Imperial authorities to come down on this planet hard. It would have been the end of New America's privileged self-governing status."

Her eyes flashed pale fire. "Maybe that at least would have shown our people what a sham it had been all along, and provoked them to resist!"

"Now you're talking like the Sons of bloody Wilkinson—terrorist logic!" Rogers stopped abruptly, annoyed with himself for letting his flash of temper show through years of carefully cultivated professional impassivity. But he had never been able to entirely suppress his irritation at the readiness with which intelligent people abdicated the right and duty of thought in favor of ideological sloganeering. His self-annoyance caused his voice to go cold. "Anyway, whatever happens, your position in NAISA is safe. I've given explicit orders that they're not to be told of your connection with the Sons of Arnold. After all, we do owe you a favor for your role in the raid on *Mayflower II*."

"I gather that I'm expected to slobber with gratitude." Her scorn was rich. "You'll always be able to hold over me the threat of revealing it. And next I suppose you're going to tell me that I won't be permanently under surveillance by Lieutenant Commander—oh, excuse me, I mean *Assistant Secretary* Logan!"

"No, I won't insult your intelligence by pretending that. But can you really blame us? And you'll have no cause for concern as long as you keep your nose clean."

For an instant, he thought she was going to try to strike him. The two security men behind her evidently thought the same thing, for they moved a little closer to her from each side.

At that moment, the communicator in Logan's car beeped for attention. Logan acknowledged and, after a brief exchange, called to Rogers with a puzzled frown.

"Commander, someone wants to talk to you. It's on the NAISA wavelength, but it obviously isn't them."

"Can you give me a visual?" asked Rogers, turning to the car.

"Right. This is a specially equipped car." Logan activated a small screen on the dashboard.

"Rogers speaking. Who is this?"

The screen came to life, and Rogers found himself looking into the face of Ethan Stark.

"Surprised that I know you're out there?" he sneered. "One of the martyrs aboard *Mayflower II* got off a fragmentary message, which we received a short time ago. Whatever had happened, I knew you had to somehow be behind it. And we do have alarm devices covering the approaches to this headquarters."

Rogers forced calmness on himself. Out of the corner of his eye he saw that Grey had shouldered up close enough to see the screen, but she was not within the video pickup.

"Do I gather then," he asked in a steady voice, "that you're inside the headquarters?"

"Yes—and we've taken it over! The Sons of Arnold have failed. Now their weakness will be purged! We have a ship in the warehouse. We're going to take off directly from here, and carry on the struggle!"

"If you can do that, then why haven't you? Why are you wasting time bragging about it to me?"

"Because I want to make clear to you and to the crawling collaborationists of NAISA—they're receiving this too, in their command aircar—that we have hostages. If there is any pursuit by NAISA, those hostages will die." Stark moved aside, to reveal the room behind him. A cluster of people, mostly middle-aged or older, sat dejectedly on the floor, under the guns of a pair of what were presumably Sons of Wilkinson members.

Grey thrust herself into the pickup to stare at the screen. "Professor Boudreau! Mrs. Weston! And...Dr. Bricknell!"

Stark was back in the screen, and his expression had changed to one of dull hurt. "So it's you too, Grey. I was right; he's corrupted you. You've turned against everything we've ever believed in and joined the Empire."

"Ethan," she said with desperate intensity, "these people are the leaders of the Sons of Arnold. You'd never kill them. I know you wouldn't."

"No?" All at once, the betrayed lover was gone and the fanatic was back. Stark's blue eyes were like holes in a blazing furnace of hate. "I'll kill them gladly! It's their soft-headedness that's forced us to take direct action. So you see, it isn't our fault. It isn't our fault! Nothing is our fault..." He seemed about to trail off into psychotic repetition, but then his glare was back in full force. "But I see you're forcing me to prove that I mean what I say." He turned, grabbed Dr. Bricknell by the arm and dragged him closer to the pickup. The old man's gentle face, normally ruddy, was a pale gray, and wore a look too uncomprehending even to be horrified.

Stark drew a combat knife.

"Ethan! No!" screamed Grey. "You *can't*! Not Dr. Bricknell."

"Don't do it, Stark!" Rogers snapped. "We believe you. There'll be no pursuit. You don't need to—"

Stark showed no sign of having heard them. Grasping Bricknell's jaw, he pulled his head back and brought the knife across the exposed throat in a quick slash. Blood gushed, soaking Stark, who lowered the body to the floor and stared wildly from the screen.

"You *made* me do it! It wasn't my fault!"

Grey's mouth worked, but no words came. A low keening arose from one of the female hostages; otherwise, they all seemed frozen into a group sculpture entitled "Shock." Even the two guards gave Stark troubled glances—but they kept their weapons on line.

"Now you know I mean business," Stark was continuing. "I'll kill the rest of them if I'm pursued. I had to prove it. So it was your fault. It wasn't my fault."

The repetition was beginning to tell on Rogers. In fact, sheer irritation brought him out of stunned paralysis. "All right. You've made your point. But tell me something," he added, remembering that he had to extract as much information from this lunatic as possible. "Where, exactly, do you imagine you can go? There's nowhere you'll be safe."

"That's what *you* think," said Stark with a leer of mad triumph. "We're going to the Gharnakh station. The Gharnakh'sha have offered us sanctuary—us and Malani, who's still there. They've also offered to take us to one of their worlds, where we'll be beyond your reach."

The Gharnakh'sha are probably telling the truth, thought Rogers. *Giving these people a secure base from which to hatch plots can only help them in their efforts to undermine the Empire. Historically, embittered exiles have often been used that way.*

"Stark, I've got some bad news for you. Captain Viglione at Washington Station has already ordered his ships to proceed to the Gharnakh station."

"And of course Viglione wouldn't give a damn about our hostages. They're mere New Americans, aren't they? But take a look at the astronomy of the thing, Commander. They can't possibly intercept us before we get there."

"But once they arrive, they're going to reduce that station to its component atoms if it doesn't surrender. The fact that Malani is there ought to provide added motivation."

Stark gave him a sly smirk. "Ah, but there's something that may come as news to *you!*" Before Rogers could try to elicit the nature of that something, Stark's expression closed up and he spoke harshly. "Enough talk! We're leaving. You NAISA lickspittles—I know you're listening—won't pursue us. You're still New Americans, however much you've betrayed your heritage, and so are our hostages." The screen went blank.

Rogers looked at Grey, who had not made a sound since Dr. Bricknell's murder. A single tear was trickling down her cheek. It was the only sign of life or motion in a face that might have been that of a marble sculpture.

A humming, rumbling sound came from the warehouse. From its rear side, a spacecraft rose on grav repulsion and swooped away into the sky. From the glimpse he got, Rogers could tell it was a Voyager class, probably the same one Stark had been using before—the largest Bernheim Drive–capable vessel that could have fit into the warehouse's interior as Rogers remembered it. As soon as hardwired safety interlocks permitted, its photon rockets came to life and it climbed aloft at a steep angle of attack. Soon it was nothing but a point of bright light.

"Shall we check that place out, Commander?" asked Logan.

"No. I have feeling that—"

At once, Rogers' feeling was confirmed. The front wall of the warehouse exploded outward with a roar, followed by a series of secondary explosions that brought the entire building crashing down. They rose from the ground where they had instinctively flattened themselves and stared across the open area at a pile of rubble.

"I wonder if anybody was still alive in there?" Logan said aloud.

Without comment, Rogers turned to the command car. "Get me Resident Commissioner Tewari," he ordered the communications operator.

✧   ✧   ✧

"...And of course we have no naval vessels here to follow him," Tewari concluded his gloomy assessment after Rogers had brought him up to date.

"And we, of course, have only orbital capability," added NAISA Assistant Director Nathanial Mason, perhaps a bit pointedly.

"What we do have is the Rover I came here in," said Rogers. "I can follow him. Just give me a few security men."

"But the hostages—" Mason began.

"I can probably track him without him being aware of it—besides being a very small craft, the Rover has a highly capable stealth suite. And I'll be using passive gravitic sensors."

"Ah...isn't that a bit hazardous?" Tewari wondered.

"Commissioner, I believe this falls within the purview of my investigation here, and within my authority in connection with that mission. I must reserve the right to use my own judgment."

"But what do you expect to accomplish with a small, unarmed vessel?"

"I don't know," Rogers admitted forthrightly. "I'll just have to see how the situation develops and play it by ear. That's why I asked for the security men, against any possible eventualities. But at a minimum I can shadow him and make sure he really is going to the Gharnakh station and wasn't merely lying to us. Also, I can be there when Captain Viglione's ships arrive. Stark was unfortunately correct about their inability to prevent him from getting there." He smiled wryly. "I wasn't being altogether candid with Stark about their mission. They may or may not be able to attack the station without reinforcements from Sol. That, too, is something on which we'll have to act as seems indicated. But whatever happens, I want to be there for it."

"I'd like to come too, Commander," said Logan.

"Is that all right with you, Commissioner?"

"Yes," said Tewari, nodding in the screen. "I'll arrange for the Rover to be prepared for immediate takeoff. Good luck!" He signed off.

"Let's go," Rogers told Logan. "Bring two of your best men. There's no time to waste."

"I'm going too," Grey stated flatly. After so long a silence, the sound of her voice was almost startling.

Rogers turned and faced her. "Are you sure you want to come

with me?" he asked with a smile. "I thought you had decided I'm some kind of monster."

"There are monsters and there are monsters. Ethan Stark is the latter. And now I understand the difference between the two."

She turned on her heel and walked toward the glide car. Rogers could only follow.

CHAPTER TWENTY-ONE

TEWARI WAS AS GOOD AS HIS WORD. WHEN THE GLIDE CAR, DRIVEN at reckless speed by Logan, came screaming onto the tarmac alongside the terminal, the last consignment of supplies was being loaded aboard the Rover. The resident commissioner had also taken care of clearance; there were neither delays nor interference as they soared aloft. Rogers engaged the Bernheim Drive in sublight mode closer to New America's Primary Limit than standard safety procedures mandated, to save time. It was well he did so, for they barely had time to establish a sensor lock on Stark's ship, headed above the plane of the ecliptic, before it passed the nearby Secondary Limit of Tau Ceti, formed its warp field, and went transluminal.

Rogers had suspected that Stark would try a faster-than-light hop (which should take just under four and a half seconds) out to somewhere above the debris disk in the region of the Gharnakh station, to which he would then proceed under slower-than-light pseudo-acceleration. He resolved to do the same, wondering as he did the precise calculations how many more times he could press his luck—he was beating the odds already—and not wildly overshoot his destination. The fact that they would be skirting the immediate vicinity of the local sun wouldn't help. *Just one more time*, he thought. *That's all I ask. Then back to nice, safe, conservative piloting for me.*

153

Of course he had no way of knowing exactly where Stark intended to emerge from warp, but he didn't need to know it. Afterwards, his quarry would have to thread its way through the debris disk at a cautious slower-than-light pace and shed its pseudovelocity as it approached its destination, all of which should allow time to reacquire a fix on it. He decided to err on the side of caution and aim for a point somewhat short of optimal. Even given the limited intrinsic velocity of New America's orbit plus what his photon rockets had built up short of the Primary Limit, backtracking would be tedious.

Coming out of warp after a disconcerting four and a half seconds, he saw with a sigh of relief that his luck had held. He was where he wanted to be, and it almost immediately became apparent that Stark had not been lying about his destination. His ship was proceeding through the debris disk—under sublight Bernheim Drive because reaction drive would have taken too long, but with great caution—toward the point his computer told him the Gharnakh station should now occupy in its orbit around distant Tau Ceti. With equal caution, Rogers followed. There was no rush, for Stark would have to use photon thrusters to match vectors with the station once he got there, a time-consuming process.

"I wonder what makes him think he's going to find refuge there?" Rogers wondered aloud. "He knows that station is earmarked for destruction."

"Well," said Logan, seated to his right, "you know what General Bonaparte once said."

"Quite a few things, as I recall." The French officer, who had served the monarchy in the decades following the Comte de Mirabeau's reforms, was still remembered as a brilliant military theoretician and a maker of trenchant aphorisms. "What, specifically?"

"He said, 'Never interrupt your enemy when he is making a mistake.'"

Rogers grinned. "I have no intention of interrupting him, or even letting him know I'm here. We'll do our own vector-matching and then remain just inside sensor range and see if any ships leave that station. In the meantime, we can go ahead and let Tewari and Captain Viglione know he and Malani are there. Otherwise, we simply wait for the ships from Washington Station to arrive."

"How long will that be?" asked Grey, from Rogers' left.

"I don't know. They departed at about the same time we did. But they're coming sublight and they've got a long way to come." Rogers did a quick check on the astrogation computer. "Twenty-six astronomical units, in fact. Those are fast ships, but they're proceeding cautiously because their entire course lies within the debris disk."

"Can't naval force screens cope with the smaller asteroidal rubble?"

"Yes, but you know what a collision with any of the big rocks can do to the drive."

"Maybe they went above the ecliptic to avoid that," Logan suggested hopefully.

"That would have been the smart move," Rogers agreed. "But regardless, we wait."

As it turned out, avoiding the dense plane of the debris disk was precisely what Commander Ian Forsythe, skipper of HMSS *Rooke* and by-courtesy-so-called commodore of Washington Station's tiny flotilla, had done. So, at a pseudo-acceleration of around four hundred gravities, he didn't make Rogers and his companions wait too long.

The wait gave Rogers a chance to become better acquainted with the two security men Logan had brought. Both were North Americans. David Villa was from the Dominion of Texas, and his face showed evidence of both Spanish and Indian blood. He was a lively sort, unlike the stocky, taciturn Adam Kovac, a native of the Dominion of Indiana. They had come equipped only with sidearms, of which each had two: a stunner, and a Gauss needler in case stronger discouragement was called for. Logan vouched for their competence, and Rogers found no reason to doubt it.

While they waited, they subjected the Gharnakh station to as detailed an examination as they could manage while continuing to conceal their own presence. They found nothing to contradict the impression Rogers had formed on the basis of the bare glimpse he had gotten while escaping from it. Although assembling it clandestinely, even out here in the wastes of the debris disk, must have been a major project, it wasn't very large in any absolute sense. And its defensive armament was no more formidable than he had thought. He began to feel confident that *Rooke* and her smaller companions would be able to deal with it unaided.

At the same time, something began to bother him. Stark's ship had berthed itself in the same hangar bay Rogers remembered—and he remembered it well enough to know it wouldn't hold much more than that. And there were no ships of any kind moored outside the station. How, then, did the Gharnakh'sha intend to keep their promise to transport their human associates Stark and Malani from the Tau Ceti system to a Gharnakh world? Stark's *Voyager* might in theory be up to a very long interstellar trip, but it would be miserably overcrowded with Malani and his men aboard as well as Stark and his. It certainly wouldn't be able to carry any Gharnakh crew in addition, even if it had possessed accommodations adapted to their species.

"Maybe they have no intention of keeping their promise," suggested Grey when he mentioned it.

"Maybe. But Stark would have reached the same conclusions I have—he's crazy but not stupid—and he came straight here anyway. I wonder if he knows something we don't know."

They were still wondering when Forsythe's command arrived.

HMSS *Rooke* was a Benbow-class fifth-rater—what was sometimes called a "frigate," although it was precisely to avoid confusion with the old terminology of wet-navy ship types that the still-older system of rates had been revived. As such, she lacked the Bernheim Drive–equipped torpedoes (so called to distinguish them from the smaller "missiles," propelled by reaction drives), which only the mighty first- through third-rate capital ships were large enough to mount. She did, however, have launchers for missiles, intended for planetary bombardment and orbital space combat inside the Primary Limit. Outside that limit, any ship under Bernheim Drive could avoid them with contemptuous ease, but they were useable in deep space against an immobile target like the Gharnakh station. She also boasted a fairly respectable outfit of directed-energy weapons: X-ray lasers and a battery of fusion guns. The latter were short-range ship killers, using a laser battery to superheat hydrogen to a plasma state, contained in a magnetic bottle until a fusion reaction began, and then releasing it in a high-velocity star-hot jet along a laser guide beam.

Besides *Rooke*, there were three Glasgow-class sixth-raters: *Charleston*, *Madras* and *Londonderry*. These were the smallest type of deep-space warships, essentially scaled-down versions of fifth-raters but with minimal missile capability and no fusion guns. Rogers began to permit himself increasing confidence that Forsythe would be able to deal with the situation unaided.

He moved the Rover well outside sensor range of the station to rendezvous with the newcomers, having already alerted Forsythe to activate his ships' stealth suites, even though something the size of *Rooke* was, of course, harder to conceal than a small craft. As he watched the sleek, streamlined shapes—a fifth-rater was capable of atmospheric transit and planetary landing, almost the largest warship type with that capability—grow in the viewscreen, he hoped no tiresome precedence issues would arise. While they were both commanders, he had a year or so on Forsythe by date of rank. However, Forsythe was a line officer and he was not, so there was no question of him assuming command of the former's squadron. Nevertheless, this was his investigation, and he had no intention of relinquishing overall direction of it.

Deciding that a face-to-face meeting would be worthwhile despite the inconvenience, he brought the Rover, diminutive against the side of the fifth-rater, into airlock contact and went aboard *Rooke* with Grey and Logan. Commander Forsythe was an Englishman who, it seemed to Rogers, exuded by-the-book tendencies. Rogers introduced himself and Logan (using the latter's naval rank). "And this is Special Agent Grey Goldson of NAISA," he concluded, not revealing anything Forsythe would not have learned from Captain Viglione.

"Ah. Agent Goldson." Forsythe's sniff was barely perceptible, not enough to make an issue of, and his face was carefully expressionless. Rogers wasn't sure whether his problem was that Grey was a New American colonial or that she was non-Navy, or both. "Please come with me to my cabin."

Once they were seated and drinks were produced, Forsythe came to the point. "Commander Rogers, Captain Viglione has explained to me that you have been sent to this system with full authority to investigate inimical Caliphate activities and any possible...local involvement." He glanced significantly at Grey.

"Agent Goldson," said Rogers quietly, "is the liaison officer assigned to me by the New American government. She has been working closely with me over the entire course of my investigation." *True, in a sense,* he told himself. "I have complete confidence in her."

"Of course, of course! I never meant to imply—"

"Furthermore, Commander," Grey cut in rather frostily, disregarding through ignorance of naval tradition (or at least Rogers hoped that was all it was) Forsythe's right to be addressed as "Captain" aboard the ship he commanded, "the Gharnakh'sha are intruders in *our* planetary system. New America has a very real stake in this, and a right to be involved in your operations."

"No doubt. Quite." Forsythe cleared his throat and changed the subject. "At any rate, Commander Rogers, even though the discovery of the Gharnakh'sha has, shall we say, expanded the scope of this affair, Captain Viglione feels that your grant of authority from the Admiralty still covers the operation in its entirety. He has therefore ordered me to cooperate with you to the fullest and give great weight to your recommendations." He smiled and raised his glass. "Incidentally, that was a bloody good show you put on aboard *Mayflower II*."

"Thank you." Rogers was moderately relieved. Forsythe had carefully phrased his little speech so as to avoid any relinquishment of operational control of his squadron. But Viglione had made clear to him that that squadron was Rogers' instrument—he'd been unable to disguise that. And now he even seemed to be making what Rogers suspected was his best effort at being ingratiating. He raised his glass in turn.

"So, then," Forsythe resumed, "how do you propose we proceed?"

"For the moment, we should proceed cautiously and continue to keep that station under observation. I assume that Captain Viglione has shared with you the update we sent him, so you know that Stark and Malani are both there, and that Stark has hostages."

Forsythe's expression reflected what he thought of the hostage value of Sons of Arnold leaders, but he held his peace.

"In addition," Rogers continued, "they aren't going anywhere at the moment. All they've got is that Voyager of Stark's, and it's still inside the station."

"Perhaps we should reveal ourselves and issue a surrender demand, before they can try to escape."

"Actually, I hope they do try to escape; your sixth-raters can catch the Voyager, and it would be interesting to see its heading. Right now, we're under no pressure to do anything."

Forsythe started to say something, but his desk communicator beeped for attention. He frowned. "I gave the first officer orders we were not to be interrupted except for emergencies." He flicked a switch. "What is it, Number One?"

"Captain, we have a sensor reading." The female voice held what Rogers recognized as the lilt of Antilia, Gamma Leoporis VI, a terraformed world colonized mainly by people from the Dominion of the West Indies. It also held strain. "Unidentified ships have come out of warp and are approaching on a bearing from below the plane of the ecliptic."

For an instant, they all stared at each other. Then, with a crisp "Sound general quarters," Forsythe signed off and strode toward the bridge.

"Patrick, get back aboard our boat and stand by for immediate departure," Rogers ordered Logan. "Grey, come with me." The two of them followed Forsythe.

"What was that about no pressure?" Grey muttered as they hurried along the passageways of a warship coming to full readiness.

CHAPTER TWENTY-TWO

"CAPTAIN'S ON THE BRIDGE!" INTONED A MARINE SENTRY, AND A female lieutenant commander of obvious African descent and willowy build—Rogers recalled that Antilia was a low-gravity world—immediately relinquished the captain's chair.

"All right, Mr. Willis," said Forsythe. "Bring me up to date."

"As you see, sir," said Willis. She pointed to a holographic display covering the immediate region of the debris disk as Rogers and Grey looked over Forsythe's shoulders. "They don't seem to be employing any sort of stealth, which is why our long-range sensors were able to pick them up even though they're on the far side of the debris disk from us."

"They wouldn't," said Rogers grimly.

Forsythe turned in his chair to face him. "What do you mean?"

Instead of answering him directly, Rogers addressed the first officer. "Commander Willis, have you been able to identify these ships?"

"No, sir. We've been able to get mass readings for them, but their energy signatures don't match any ship classes in our database."

"So I thought." Rogers turned back to Forsythe. "Those are Gharnakh ships—they've got to be. The course they're following, from below the ecliptic, tells us roughly the direction to the Gharnakh'sha Unity—and it squares with what I'd already learned, that they're in Eridanus, as viewed from Earth." *Assuming that R'Ghal wasn't lying to us*, he mentally hedged. *And it begins to look as though he wasn't.* "And they're coming to evacuate that station."

"How do you know that?" demanded Forsythe. "And why are they arriving at this particular time, when we're here? It seems an incredible coincidence."

"Not at all. You see, they knew when the Sons of Wilkinson intended to put their plan into effect. After that, the station would have served its purpose, and could be abandoned and probably destroyed with great thoroughness. It was all planned in advance. And Stark knew about it. That's why he came out here: He knew he could count on transportation to the Gharnakh worlds." Rogers paused to reflect. "I expect these ships are a little behind schedule. Stark knew you wouldn't be able to prevent him from reaching the station, and he probably thought he'd be gone from this system before you arrived. As it is . . . Mr. Willis, please rotate that holo-display."

Willis complied, and Rogers studied it and its accompanying readouts. "All right. We're above the plane of the ecliptic, just outside the denser regions of the debris disk. They're below it—and somewhat further from it, as you would expect, since they naturally wanted to be entirely outside the debris disk when they came out of warp. And the station is almost dead center in the heart of the debris disk, so they're having to proceed toward it cautiously. This gives us the opportunity to intercept them shortly before they reach the station."

Forsythe looked worried. "Number One, I believe you mentioned that you have mass readings for those ships."

"Yes, sir." Willis brought the figures up on a display screen. Forsythe studied them and looked even more worried.

"Hmm . . . five ships intermediate in mass between our fifth- and sixth-raters. . . . One that's comparable to a fourth-rater . . . and four that are the mass of a third-rater." Forsythe swung his chair around and glared at Rogers. "Third-raters—capital ships! And one other that's equivalent to our largest cruiser-type classes! Do you seriously expect me to take on that weight of metal with the force I've got? It would be sheer suicide."

"Captain," said Rogers mollifyingly, "you're thinking exclusively in terms of warship tonnages. A third-rater masses roughly the same as a large transport. And *that* is what those four big ships really are."

"What makes you so sure?"

"In the first place, that's what they *have* to be if I'm right about their intentions. They need transports to haul away all their personnel and all the equipment of value aboard the station; warships aren't designed for that kind of work. In the second place, it would account for the fact that they seem to be moving more slowly than simple caution in the debris disk would account for—assuming, that is, that their transports, like ours, aren't built for speed like warships. And finally . . . one thing I've learned about the Gharnakh'sha is that they're not interested in a direct military confrontation with us. Their plan is to use cat's-paws like the Caliphate and the Sons of Wilkinson to undermine us from within."

"Yes, yes, I've read your report. But—"

"Don't you see? They'd have no reason to send capital ships here unless they intended such a confrontation. And if they *were* out to conquer the Tau Ceti system, or something like that, they'd send a larger force than this one."

Forsythe started to open his mouth, then closed it and looked thoughtful.

"Anyway," Rogers continued, pressing his advantage, "doesn't it seem to you like an odd, top-heavy composition for a task group? Four capital ships, and with just one cruiser type, and just five of some kind of escort class. No: I say the four big ships are cargo and passenger haulers, and the six smaller ones are here just in case they need an escort. They probably don't expect to need one—remember, when these plans were laid, they had no reason to think anyone on our side knew about the station's existence—but the Gharnakh'sha are cautious by temperament."

Forsythe scowled. "Even assuming you're right about the big ships being noncombatants, the others still outnumber us six to four, and out-mass us by a considerably higher margin than that. Of course, we don't know what sort of armament they carry—"

"No, we don't. But I'm certain that it's no more advanced or compact or efficient than ours, and I'm willing to bet that it's somewhat less so."

"What are you willing to bet? The lives of my personnel?"

"Captain, having read my report, you know I've seen some of their technology close up. It's been stagnated at our present-day level for thousands of years. Now, after having entered the Industrial Revolution only about five hundred years ago, we're already pulling ahead of them, which is the very reason they're trying to slow our advancement by promoting a technophobic society like the Caliphate. Furthermore, their entire race has been locked into a unitary state for just as long. For all those millennia, there've been no separate sovereignties among them, hence no military competition; their space navy must be more like a glorified police force. In fact, R'Ghal—you read about him in my report—admitted as much to me."

"That's why they're afraid of us," Grey put in. Then, in a tone of voice that any normal male would have found very persuasive indeed: "You can be the one to show them they have reason to be afraid!"

"Also," Rogers pressed on, "think of your tactical advantage. That's not a fighting fleet out there, it's a convoy. *You* don't have any defenseless transports to protect!"

Forsythe, visibly wavering, raised one more objection. "But what if Stark and Malani slip away in their Voyager while we're too occupied to notice their departure or do anything about it?"

"That's where we come in," said Rogers. "Watching the station for that eventuality will be our job, in the Rover. It's got no business in a space battle anyway. And given its low mass and capable stealth suite, it can lurk pretty close to the station without being detected."

Forsythe shook his head. "It's too dangerous in that unarmed small craft. I'll detach one of my sixth-raters to keep the station under observation."

"No, you're going to need all your sixth-raters in battle. As you yourself have pointed out, you're outnumbered." Rogers smiled. "Besides, you're going to have to let the Rover go anyway; clinging to the hull the way it is now, it would degrade *Rooke*'s performance. Since it will be on its own, it may as well be doing something useful."

Forsythe scowled. "I still don't like it. Damn me if I do."

Rogers sighed and chose his words carefully. "Captain Forsythe, I remind you that I have plenary authority, direct from the Admiralty, in matters involving subversion in this system by the Caliphate and disaffected local elements, which Malani and Stark between them personify. You are in tactical command of this squadron, but as regards the overall conduct of the investigation I must stand on that grant of authority, and reserve the right to use my own judgment."

"I might add," Grey chimed in, "that Stark is culpable under New American law for any number of crimes, most recently the murder of Dr. Elihu Bricknell, which I personally witnessed. As a

New American law enforcement officer—the only one present—I have a responsibility to make certain he does not escape from our jurisdiction. Therefore it is essential that I accompany Commander Rogers."

"I quite agree," said Rogers. Privately, it occurred to him that if Stark came to trial, his testimony would expose Grey's double role, which at a minimum would end her career in NAISA.

Of course, there was a simple solution for that...

"But," Forsythe protested, "I say, if Stark and Malani do try to make good an escape, what can you two do in that unarmed vessel? You can alert us, but we're likely to be altogether too busy to take any action."

"In that event," said Rogers, "we will follow them and ascertain their destination. Our Rover is as fast as their Voyager, and it has a sensor suite that's adequate for keeping a lock on a ship it's pursuing faster than light. We'll follow them wherever they go."

"But they expect to find refuge in Gharnakh space. What if—?"

"Wherever they go," Rogers repeated firmly, emphasizing each syllable.

"I concur," said Grey quietly.

For a silent moment, Forsythe looked at one of them and then the other. When he spoke, all he said was, "You'd better get cracking. Good luck."

The Rover cut its airlock connection to *Rooke* and peeled away. The warships realigned themselves and sped away under slower-than-light Bernheim Drive, plunging into the debris disk at the maximum prudent acceleration. Rogers kept formation with them.

"One thing you forgot to mention to Forsythe," said Grey, sitting beside him on the tiny bridge.

"What was that?" asked Rogers, who thought he had a pretty good idea of what it was.

"Judging from that holo-display, his course to intercept those incoming ships is going to bring him fairly close to the Gharnakh station before he comes in contact with them."

"Don't worry. He won't come anywhere near close enough to be in range of the station's weapons."

"That wasn't what I was thinking of. I don't have the figures, but I imagine he *will* pass the station too closely for any stealth features to conceal the presence of ships the size of his."

"Your instinct is accurate. So the station will be able to alert their ships that he's coming—if they haven't already detected his ships, which they probably will have."

"Probably. But the point is, Stark and Malani will know that their transportation has been discovered and is about to come under attack. It may stampede them into going ahead and trying to make a getaway on their own."

"Not necessarily," Rogers demurred. "Maybe, given the imbalance of forces involved, they'll assume the Gharnakh'sha will be victorious."

"I think you mentioned earlier that Stark is crazy but not stupid. I suspect that the same holds true of Malani."

"Well, we'll just have to get in position before that can happen."

Soon, they separated from Forsythe's formation and set a new course, applying a deceleration calculated to nullify their pseudovelocity just before coming so close to the station that even the Rover's sophisticated stealth could not hide them. Rogers didn't risk a farewell-and-best-wishes to *Rooke* as she led her trio of smaller sisters onward toward battle. Instead, he checked his sensors, which by now could pick up the Gharnakh ships, and did a quick calculation with the help of the astrogation computer. It appeared that the newcomers were going to come further than he had previously thought before Forsythe could intercept them. In other words, the engagement was going to take place closer to the station—and the Rover—than expected.

Well, he philosophized, *we'll have a ringside seat.*

Leaving the ship on autopilot, he stepped down to the central cabin, where Logan, Kovac and Villa waited patiently. Their departure had been too hurried for any explanations, and he had been dreading the prospect of telling them in detail what they were getting into. After all, they hadn't precisely signed on to face the possibility of leaving the Tau Ceti system. But now he told all. The three men evinced somberness (even Villa's usual animation was in abeyance) but, to Rogers' relief, also steadiness.

"Well, Pat," he said to Logan afterwards with a smile, "do you have a quote from General Bonaparte to cover what we're trying, which I wouldn't blame you for thinking is impossible?"

"Actually, I do. He once said, 'Impossible is a word to be found only in the dictionary of fools.'"

CHAPTER TWENTY-THREE

SHORTLY AFTER THEY HAD PARTED COMPANY, FORSYTHE'S COM-
mand passed within the envelope of space where the Gharnakh
station could not help but detect it, and undoubtedly transmitted
the information to the incoming flotilla. Rogers watched anxiously,
and finally breathed what he hoped was a not-too-conspicuous
sigh of relief, for he had just been proved correct about the
composition of that flotilla. If those four big ships had in fact
been capital ships comparable to the Empire's third-raters, and
if the Gharnakh'sha shared human ideas about armament mixes,
then Forsythe's crews would now be staring at onrushing salvos
of long-range torpedoes accelerating at hundreds of gees under
Bernheim Drive and detonating to produce ravening bomb-
pumped X-ray lasers. But no such torpedoes had appeared. The
two formations simply continued toward each other, closing the
distance. This battle would be fought "at push of pike," or what
passed for it in space warfare.

He had already explained all this to Grey, who wasn't Navy.
Now she seemed to read his thoughts. "Nice to know that we
didn't condemn Forsythe and his people to death," she said drily.

"We hope," he muttered, distracted, as he watched the display.
All the encouraging arguments he had made to Forsythe had
been sincere and perfectly valid, but the fact remained that the

largest Gharnakh warship was equivalent to an Imperial fourth-rater, sometimes referred to as a "heavy frigate," and therefore outweighed *Rooke*. And the five smaller hostiles were somewhat bigger than Forsythe's three sixth-raters. *Call them six-and-a-half-raters*, he thought, with what he hoped wasn't gallows humor. He could only try to reassure himself with the same reasoning he had used to persuade Forsythe.

Applying as little power as possible, he eased the Rover as close to the station as he could and still lurk undetected, with the Gharnakh'sha's attention presumably riveted on the impending class of warships. His passive sensors reported no activity around the station, and certainly no departures.

"Evidently," said Grey, "Stark and Malani have looked at the balance of forces and are not panicking."

"I trust their confidence is unwarranted...although if it begins to look as though it is, they'll undoubtedly try to make a break in their Voyager while they still have a chance, before Forsythe can finish off the Gharnakh ships and get back here and demand the surrender of the station."

She cocked an eyebrow at him. "And if it turns out their confidence *is* warranted...?"

"Then the victorious Gharnakh will take them away as originally planned. And there'll be nobody out here to ascertain the exact location of their sanctuary planet except us."

"So what you're trying to tell me is that no matter which side wins we're committed to following them wherever they go." It was a statement, not a question.

"Yes, I suppose that is what I'm saying." He turned to face her squarely. "Are you sorry you came along?"

Her eyes slid away. "No," she said quietly. "What I said to Forsythe was true. This is my job. But it goes beyond what I told him; I don't just mean my official job. It's something I have to do."

Hmm...Is it possible that she needs to do this as a form of expiation? That she's come to see that the Sons of Wilkinson were inevitable all along because the idealism of the Sons of Arnold has always been open-ended in the direction of violence, and that now she's trying to atone for having been associated with it? Or is it merely her way of wiping out her shame for having been duped by Ethan Stark? Rogers decided to keep the questions to himself, for anything he said would probably be counterproductive.

Instead, he asked, smiling, "Even though you're having to do it in association with me?"

She gave him a sidelong glance. "One can't always be too choosy about one's allies." Then, with a humorless laugh: "I suppose you think that makes me sound like the Sons of Wilkinson again."

"Not really. You're not taking that philosophy to the extremes they do. After all, you must admit I'm not as bad as the Caliphate or the Gharnakh'sha."

"Maybe." Her smile was brief, but it was a smile.

As the two naval forces drew closer to each other, the Rover's sensor equipment and its cybernetic brain provided a holographic display of their maneuvers, with friendlies as icons of green and hostiles as red ones, with the four big transports following some distance behind a protective screen of warships. Rogers instructed the brain to sound a warning if any activity was observed at the Gharnakh station, and they all clustered around the holo-cube, which they regarded gravely.

As they watched, a pair of the "six-and-a-half-raters" detached themselves from the scarlet formation and dropped back toward the transports, which they flanked. No surprise, thought Rogers; the Gharnakh commander was being cautious in guarding his charges, even if it meant dividing his forces. Then, before the opposing ships came into laser weapons range, the green icons altered course, increased their acceleration and, with the kind of maneuvering possible to spacecraft under slower-than-light Bernheim Drive, swerved around as though to come in behind the shielding warships to attack the transports. The Gharnakh commander had, of course, seen the same thing, and his ships swung raggedly about to counter the move and protect the lightly guarded noncombatant ships. In the process, their formation unavoidably lost its coherence.

"When I wish to give battle, my enemy, even though protected by high walls and deep moats, cannot help but engage me, for I attack a position he must succor," Rogers mentally quoted Sun Tzu. He began to revise his opinion of Forsythe. The man might be a walking stereotype of a certain kind of Limey, but as a naval officer he evidently knew his business.

The two squadrons, now equal in numbers, slid together in the holo-display, and the icons began to blink with indicia of damage as the duel of X-ray lasers—the only kind of lasers energetic enough to be effective at space-combat ranges—began. In the early days of space flight, it had been believed that such lasers could never be more than single-shot weapons because the only way to generate one was by detonating a fusion bomb. Then a way had been found to produce an X-ray laser pulse by using a free electron laser to ionize carbon material, the resultant plasma undergoing population inversion and giving off coherent X-rays. It had taken time before the technology had been up to translating this principle into gigawatt weapon-grade lasers. But in the present era, though practically useless in atmosphere (which absorbs X-rays), they were the standard medium-range weapons of ship-to-ship combat. Now those invisible but extremely high-intensity energy pulses were crisscrossing the rapidly diminishing space separating the Imperial and Gharnakh ships, whose shields of immaterial force would be struggling to nullify the devastating energy transfer when they struck. The screens were not always successful, and damage control parties would be frantically at work.

But as they watched, the shamrock-green icon representing *Rooke* drove inexorably in, apparently heedless of damage.

"Forsythe wants to close to within fusion gun range of that Gharnakh fourth-rater," said Logan.

"Isn't that reckless?" asked Grey anxiously.

"It's risky," Logan acknowledged. "But I think I know how Forsythe's mind is working. He's inferred from the volume of laser fire that fourth-rater is putting out that it can't have room for many short-range ship smashers."

"There's something else," said Rogers, not taking his eyes off the display. "I think he's counting on the fact that the Gharnakh'sha haven't fought a war against a serious enemy for thousands of years, and betting that their plasma weapons are going to be equivalent to our older ones, and to the portable squad-support versions our Marines still use. In other words, they aren't going to contain the plasma in the magnetic bottle quite long enough for it to reach fusion temperatures, and therefore are going to be a good deal less destructive."

As he closely scrutinized the display, Rogers noticed something else again. Unless he was mistaken, the Gharnakh ships' maneuvering seemed to be somewhat more sluggish than Forsythe's. The RSN's helmsmen were selected for their ability to use direct neural computer interfacing to make their ships extensions of their own bodies. The same was true of other human space navies, save that of the Caliphate, whose mullahs had forbidden it as contrary to the will of Allah. He doubted that the Gharnakh'sha had any such religious scruples, but he wondered if perhaps they hadn't developed the capability before freezing their technology—or simply lacked, as a species, the talent to use it effectively, which was fairly rare even among humans.

As they watched, the large green and red icons drew so close together as to almost touch in a display of this scale—the Gharnakh commander wasn't avoiding close-range battle, perhaps trusting in his ship's superior size—and the readouts began to go wild with damage assessments. Rogers tried to visualize the scene. The fusion guns' "ammunition" consisted of power cartridges which served as liners for the magnetic bottles containing the plasma. Recoil energy activated a purge cycle in which the blazing-hot spent cartridge (or what was left of it) was ejected into space. These were brutal, clumsy weapons; the firing process was deafeningly noisy and stupefyingly hot, despite all that cooling systems could do. It caused the ship to reel and shudder, and unlike the invisible X-ray lasers the discharge was blinding. For *Rooke*'s crew, it was an experience only to be compared to being on the gun deck of an eighteenth-century man-of-war.

He was still trying to imagine it when the red icon began to flicker, and then went out. Nobody cheered or whooped; there were only five sighs of relief. In his mind's eye, Rogers saw the Gharnakh ship, a ship larger than *Rooke,* bulging outward from internal secondary explosions, with great rents tearing open in its sides to reveal hellfire, before its powerplant went critical and it vanished in a sunlike fireball around which a cloud of white-hot vapor rapidly dissipated. Space warfare differed from all other forms of armed conflict in that the killed vastly outnumbered the merely wounded, such was the almost inconceivable lethality of the forces at play. If you weren't hale and healthy aboard a sound ship, you were probably dead.

He ran his eye over the rest of the display. The smaller ships were engaged in laser duels, and the Imperial ones were at least holding their own. They were smaller than their opponents, but appeared to be more maneuverable, and that combined with what seemed to be superior targeting meant they were scoring more hits. One of them, HMSS *Charleston*, had been destroyed, but so

had one of the Gharnakh ones, and a second was showing crip-
pling damage. And now *Rooke* began to add its laser fire, and
the damaged Gharnakh ship's icon began to flicker. The relatively
undamaged one began to pull back toward the diamond-shaped
formation of transports and their two small escorts. *Rooke*, *Madras*
and *Londonderry* followed, leaving the almost certainly doomed
Gharnakh cripple to its fate. Rogers didn't know whether or not
the three remaining "six-and-a-half-raters" were fast enough to
leave Forsythe's command behind in a stern chase and get outside
the debris disk where they could safely form their warp fields
and escape. But even if they were, they couldn't do so without
leaving the lumbering, defenseless transports behind.

"Whoever's in command of the Gharnakh'sha now will have
to either fight or strike his colors," said Logan, using a very old
naval expression.

"My thought as well, with the caveat that I doubt very much
he'll do the latter," said Rogers with a nod. "But we're probably not
the only ones who're thinking it."

At that instant, as though on cue, a nerve-jarring alarm sounded.

Rogers manipulated controls, and the holo-image of the battle
was replaced by one of the Gharnakh station and its vicinity. A
small red icon had separated from the station and was drawing
away. He didn't need to summon up mass and energy-emission
readings to know what that icon represented.

"They've realized that they aren't going to be picked up
according to plan," he stated, "and that the station is next. So
they've decided their only chance is a getaway in their Voyager,
however overcrowded it may be."

"And Forsythe still has a battle to finish," Grey added.

"So..." Rogers hesitated. Legally, he could simply order Logan
and his men to participate in what he intended to do. But they
had, he decided, passed beyond legalities. So he looked around,
meeting each pair of eyes in turn. "Are we all agreed?"

Everyone nodded.

"Pat," Rogers told Logan, "send Forsythe a message—a very
brief squirt, to minimize the chance of giving away our presence—
informing him of our intentions." He then turned to the astrogation display. The little red icon was dim and fluctuating, which
meant that the escapees had activated their stealth suite. He
studied their course.

Grey was studying it too. "They're not heading in the direction the Gharnakh ships came from," she observed.

"Of course not. That would bring them too close to the battle—close enough for Forsythe to detect them. No, they'll have to circle around the battlespace, far enough from it for their stealth to conceal them from Forsythe, who'll have his hands full anyway. We'll have to stay close enough for our sensors to keep a lock on them as they work their way out of the debris disk on sublight."

"Won't that enable their sensors to pick *us* up?"

"I don't think so. This is a smaller ship, with a more capable stealth suite. That gives us a margin to work within. Besides, they have no reason to think anyone is following them. I doubt if they'll pay much attention to the view-aft."

"Message sent," Logan reported.

Rogers did a mental calculation. Their separation from *Rooke* was not great as astronomical distances went. Still, it would take finite time for a lightspeed transmission to reach Forsythe, and for him to reply. Besides which, receiving the reply would double the chance of their being discovered.

"We won't wait for an acknowledgment," he decided. "Let's go."

They set out.

CHAPTER TWENTY-FOUR

IT WAS A TRUISM THAT TWO SHIPS TRAVELING AT TRANSLIGHT pseudovelocities could not exchange fire. Any form of energy projected outside the warp field would be promptly left far behind. In theory, it should have been possible to fire directly astern at a pursuing ship, but for a variety of reasons—not the least of which was the attenuating effect of the negative-energy field—this had always proven completely impractical.

Much the same factors applied to detection using active sensors. Passive sensors were another matter. To them, an active warp field stood out like a blazing beacon. But a translight ship could not use them to detect a ship following it; it, and its lightspeed-limited passive sensors, were drawing away too fast. On the other hand, a ship astern could pick up the residual images left behind by a ship ahead of it.

Which was the basis of Rogers' hopes of following Stark's Voyager. As he had told Grey, he relied on the Rover's stealth to keep them concealed while still sublight. Then, once in clear space below the debris disk and free of hazards, Stark formed his warp field and went transluminal. Watching intently, Rogers was able to do the same almost instantly, and the stealth became superfluous. Still, being a "suspenders *and* belt man" by temperament, he kept it activated and stayed as far astern as he could without losing contact with the Voyager. Maintaining that separation proved easy; both of these small vessels followed the standard commercial rule of thumb as to the percentage of their mass devoted to the Bernheim Drive, which yielded around two hundred gees of sublight acceleration and a translight pseudovelocity in the vicinity of 1900 *c*. If anything, the Rover was slightly the faster of the two. Rogers set the autopilot to the same speed as the Voyager, and instructed the Rover's small but fairly capable "brain" to sound an alarm if the range between the two ships altered by more than a very small percentage. Only then was he able to relax somewhat. Logan was technically a qualified pilot, but he was rusty, and Rogers couldn't help being nervous whenever he had to turn over the con to him. And he had to sleep sometimes.

But in fact, the removal of one worry only made room for others. For one thing, he had absolutely no idea of how long a voyage they were embarked upon.

"I don't think it will be an extremely long one," he assured Grey on the second "day."

"Why? Because R'Ghal told us that their frontier systems aren't too far outside our own sphere of exploration?"

"And therefore they know it won't be long until we discover them," Rogers nodded, finishing her thought. "Which is precisely why they're worried. But while our periphery extends as much as fifty light-years from Sol in some directions, like Auriga, it isn't really a sphere by any means. Very irregular, in fact...and it's particularly 'flat' in the region of Eridanus. Only a little over thirty light-years from Sol, and we're in unexplored territory. And, starting at Tau Ceti, we don't even have to go that far—we already have a head start in more or less the right direction.

"Also, there's something else. Stark's Voyager isn't designed for really extended operations, any more than this Rover is, and he knows it. And while it's larger than our boat, it must be more crowded, what with his men and Malani's."

"Not to mention his hostages."

"We don't know he brought them along. I suspect not—he probably left them on the Gharnakh station." *Or killed them*, Rogers carefully did not add. "He'd have no use for them among the Gharnakh'sha, and they'd just be more mouths to feed aboard ship."

The last part reminded Rogers of yet another worry. He had been grateful to discover that Sir Ranjit Tewari's last-minute reprovisioning of the Rover had included a major supplementation of its food supplies. Still, in his capacity as de facto captain, he had put the five of them on a strict rationing plan. If it came to a point where they had consumed half of their food, they would have no choice but to turn back regardless of whether or not they had accomplished their mission.

So they drove on into the depths of Eridanus. They left behind them various well-known stellar neighbors of Tau Ceti—Epsilon Eridani, an extremely young star whose gas-giant planets had no moons of any interest; 40 Eridani, a triple system whose worlds had long ago been seared clean of life when one of the components swelled into a red giant, leaving a white dwarf remnant; and 82 Eridani, whose three planets were too massive and too hot for habitability. A robot probe had discovered a potentially terraformable brown-dwarf moon around Zeta Reticuli B, at a distance of thirty-nine light-years from Sol, but so far nothing had been done about it, and the general uselessness of the systems in this direction had caused the thrust of human expansion to be diverted elsewhere to greener pastures. So only a few standard days went by before they passed beyond the pale of human activity and plunged on into the unknown.

As they did, they ascertained Stark's destination. This was easy; faster-than-light astrogation was largely a matter of point-and-shoot. So all they needed to do was project the Voyager's course out until it intersected with a star system. It did so only fifty-eight light-years from Sol—less than that from Tau Ceti—which made it obvious why the Gharnakh'sha expected the wave-front of human expansion to reach them in the near future.

Otherwise, it just added a new dimension of mystery.

"Chi Eridani," said Logan with a frown, looking over Rogers' shoulder. "Commander, this doesn't make sense."

"Why not?" asked Grey. "I know this is even closer to the periphery of human space than we expected, but—"

"That's not it," said Rogers. "Look at these readouts." He pointed at the data for Chi Eridani. It was a binary star system consisting of a G8iv star and an M-type red dwarf companion at a mean separation of 128 astronomical units.

"So...?" she asked, puzzled. "Seems pretty normal. The

companion star is too far away to be a complicating factor. And while I'm no astrophysicist, I know that the sun I grew up under is also a type G8."

"Specifically, a G8v," corrected Rogers. "The 'v' means Tau Ceti is a main-sequence star, with a steady energy output over the very long periods of time needed for its planets to become life-bearing or even potentially so. The 'iv' means Chi Eridani A is an evolving G-type subgiant." He studied the readouts. "You see: it's the same spectral type as Tau Ceti, but it's one point six times Sol's mass, four times its diameter, and puts out three hundred ninety-two times its luminosity, which is why it's a naked-eye object on Earth across fifty-eight light-years. And that luminosity has been variable over time—a fairly short time, as stellar lifespans go."

"Which means," Logan amplified, "that any moons of the one gas-giant planet that it's believed to have can't possibly be habitable."

"I see." Grey looked thoughtful. "What you're saying is that there can't be anything there to attract humans . . . or Gharnakh'sha."

"Maybe they've established a military outpost there, since they discovered us," suggested Villa, who had been listening. "An asteroid base, or a modular space station like the one in the Tau Ceti system."

"Maybe," said Rogers moodily. He glared at the tiny yellow dot of Chi Eridani in the holographic star chart as though its presence offended him. "But as I recall, Stark characterized the place he was going as a Gharnakh *world*. How can there be anything describable as a 'world' there?"

No one had an answer.

On they drove, day after day, as Tau Ceti and Sol and all the stars of human space receded astern and the yellow gleam of Chi Eridani gradually waxed in the virtual view-forward. Rogers divided their time into five watches so someone would always be watching the sensors, and could summon him if anything involving piloting should arise. The Rover's computer held a standard repertoire of entertainment and gaming, which helped to hold boredom at bay. But as time passed, crowding and tension began to take its toll on all of them.

The strain was worst for Rogers, because he was face to face with the need to decide whether or not they should continue.

Arguably, they had accomplished their minimum objective by learning where Stark and Malani were going—and, in the process, discovering the location of the nearest Gharnakh presence. And, just as arguably, their duty now was to get back safely and put that information at the disposal of the Empire's political and military leaders, who would decide how to act on it.

But Rogers' instincts argued otherwise.

Adding to his agony of indecision was the fact that he had no clear idea of what more he could accomplish with his unarmed little ship, other than perhaps finding out just exactly what it was that lurked at Chi Eridani. He fastened on the last consideration, convincing himself that the possibility of resolving that mystery justified him in continuing on. Thus he sought to rationalize his visceral unwillingness to break off the chase.

He revealed none of his inner conflict to the others. And if the same thoughts had entered their minds, no one spoke of it. This suited Rogers, who had no wish to infect his small crew with indecision. And yet . . . he would have liked to talk it over with Grey.

Increasingly, he found there were any number of things he wanted to talk over with Grey.

It was out of the question, of course, given the total lack of privacy aboard the Rover. All their conversational exchanges had to be impersonal, and largely limited to futile speculation about what awaited them at Chi Eridani and equally futile attempts to lay a plan of action once they got there.

As they drew nearer to Chi Eridani, they were able to confirm the existence of a gas-giant planet. In fact, it was a superjovian, roughly ten times the mass of Jupiter though less than twice its diameter due to gravitational compression. Like most such monster planets, it had precluded the formation of any other gas giants. And, of course, any terrestrial planets farther in would have long since been baked by their swelling sun.

On the tenth standard day, they reached Chi Eridani A's Secondary Limit—a very distant one, given the star's mass—and emulated the Voyager in going sublight. They were then able to determine more about that giant planet. Its atmosphere, powered by a searingly hot core, was turbulent. It glowed brightly in the infrared, while great auroral collars were visible across interplanetary distances. It had an array of moons, but—unusually for a gas giant of its class—no large ones. It orbited slightly outside what was, in the present era, Chi Eridani A's liquid-water zone. None of which suggested any answer to the question of what sort of Gharnakh "world" could possibly exist in this system.

But whatever it was, it was undeniably there. Stark and Malani—or, rather, the Gharnakh'sha who must surely be piloting them—certainly seemed to have no doubts about that. After compensating for the residual vector of the Gharnakh station's orbit around Tau Ceti—since none of the pseudovelocity previously attained in sublight mode was retained when the warp field was deactivated—the Voyager set a course toward the superjovian planet, whose vicinity fairly blazed with clearly artificial energy emissions, at a modest acceleration so as not to build up too much pseudovelocity that would have to be killed. They could only follow under full stealth, setting the computer to match their quarry's acceleration and trying to wring answers from their sensors.

"It's odd," said Rogers, frowning as he sat at the piloting station studying the readouts. "There seems to be an unusual concentration of those small moons in unusually distant orbits from the superjovian."

"Can we get any visual imagery on them?" asked Grey, standing behind him.

"Any time now. We should be coming close enough for the extremely long-range visual imagery to be magnified to a useful level. Right, Pat?" Rogers asked over his shoulder.

Logan, seated at the sensor station, didn't respond.

Rogers swung his seat around. Logan was staring fixedly at a screen. He noted that Villa had awakened Kovac, who had been sleeping, and that something in the air of the cabin had brought them to peer over Logan's shoulder.

"What is it, Pat?"

"Commander," said Logan expressionlessly, "I think you'd better have a look at this."

Rogers did. The highly magnified image showed the superjovian planet, with Chi Eridani A behind it and off to the side, its glare stepped down . . . and outlined against the planet, reflecting the sunlight, was . . . something else.

Grey was also looking. Rogers barely noticed that she was gripping his arm.

"And it's not just that one," Logan said. "There are others as well, in orbit around that planet. I don't know how many, just yet."

"But ... what *is* that thing, Commander?" asked Kovac. "Have you got any idea?"

"Actually, I think I do," said Rogers slowly. "And I think we can stop wondering where the Gharnakh'sha live in this system."

CHAPTER TWENTY-FIVE

THEY COULDN'T TAKE THEIR EYES OFF THE MAGNIFIED IMAGE AS it grew and grew in the screen.

It wasn't really a short cylinder. It was more like an exceptionally wide, thick wedding band, except that a tiny, glowing light source hung suspended at its geometrical center.

But all such illusions vanished as the image waxed, and that mysterious lamp's light revealed what looked unmistakably like landscape on the ring's inner surface, gleaming off what could only be bodies of water.

And yet it was undeniably an artificial construct.

And, as they watched in stunned silence, the Rover's brain proceeded in its businesslike way to ingest the sensor readings and digest them into facts and figures.

Presently, Grey became aware that Rogers was sitting at the console, studying the readouts. She dragged her eyes away from the seemingly impossible image in the viewscreen and looked over his shoulder. As the numbers unfolded, her eyes widened.

"Over twelve hundred miles in diameter," she breathed. "And over three hundred miles in width—"

"Which yields an area of just under one point two million square miles for the ring's inner surface," Rogers finished for her. "Almost equal to India."

"Bob, how could they have built such a thing?"

Bob. It was the first time she had called him that. The intimacy was a very small one. But perhaps it was a necessary one, here in the face of the unknown.

"Yes, how?" demanded Villa, with an indignation that sounded unmistakably like a barrier erected against panic. "We've been told that the Gharnakh'sha are supposed to be no more technologically advanced than we are."

"They don't need to be," said Rogers slowly. "I've seen ideas for a habitat like that before, and I've just checked the computer to confirm my recollection. Remember how we and the Dutch were about to build a space elevator a century ago, before the invention of grav repulsion made it unnecessary? It was going to be made of carbon nanotube fiber, which had recently become readily available through advances in nanotechnological manufacturing techniques. People started thinking about other possible applications, one of which was a space habitat of previously impossible size, rotating to produce artificial gravity by centrifugal force. A coil or weave of the nanotube fiber would reinforce the main bulk of the ring, whose inner surface could be given an artificial landscape, with soil, water, and atmosphere. It wouldn't even need to be roofed in; the air could be retained by an atmosphere wall about a hundred plus miles high. The only problem was that the rotation rate needed to produce one gee of angular acceleration didn't allow for much of a safety margin. And the Gharnakh'sha originated on a high-gravity planet." Rogers turned back to the computer for a moment. "I see the rotation of this one yields about zero point eight g. Maybe the Gharnakh'sha just enjoy low gravity."

"What about that . . . small artificial sun suspended in the middle?" asked Grey.

"Well, the ring is oriented with its axis or rotation perpendicular to the plane of its orbit—understandable, to avoid constantly shifting illumination effects. So Chi Eridani A is concealed from someone standing on the inner surface, and they need artificial lighting. That thing must be powered by solar panels on the outer rim of the ring, possibly supplemented by solar power satellites. I suppose it gets switched on and off for 'day' and 'night' . . . or maybe the Gharnakh'sha don't mind constant daylight.

"Anyway, the point is that it's a matter of scale, not super-advanced technology. We've had this kind of capability for a long time. We could build something like this habitat if we wanted to."

"But we never have," Logan pointed out.

"Why should we? What would be the incentive? It would be a colossal engineering project, and, like the space elevator, we just don't need it. It's a common pattern in the history of technology: an idea is conceived before it becomes practical, and by the time it *does* become practical, nobody is interested anymore because something better has come along. The only possible reason to build a habitat like this would be to create living room. And we've got plenty of that, as we expand and colonize new planets."

"The Gharnakh'sha, on the other hand, stopped expanding ten thousand years ago," said Grey.

There was a moment of thoughtful silence.

"All right," Villa persisted, "so you'd expect to find habitats like this in their major population centers. But why would they build them in a miserable, worthless system like this?"

Grey answered him before Rogers could. "Don't forget, we're talking about ten thousand years of uninterrupted, unchanging high technology. It's hard for us to fully appreciate what that means, because there's nothing to compare to it in our history. But in all that time, restricted to an arbitrary sphere in space, I imagine they've occupied and exploited every single system in that sphere that has asteroidal rubble for raw materials."

"Even a system like this, where the star is expanding so the life zone will be expanding soon?"

"Soon in terms of stellar lifespans. But in terms of human—or Gharnakh'sha—lifespans, or even civilizations..."

"They're probably not any more worried about it than we are about the fact that Earth is due to go the way of Venus in about one point seventy-five billion years," said Rogers drily.

"So," Grey resumed, "even systems like this must seem to them worth developing."

"Yes," said Rogers. "By now their total population figure must be...'astronomical' is too weak a word."

"It makes you wonder why they're even worried about us," said Logan in a dazed voice.

"R'Ghal, the Gharnakh'sha who told us about them, mentioned that their numbers and resources are overwhelming—and that they aren't counting on that. I think they're right. The invading Germanic tribes were drops in the bucket of the Roman Empire's population. A relative handful of Mongols conquered China. Old, sclerotic states can't make their manpower effective. And the Gharnakh Unity's arteries have been hardening far longer than any human empire's."

"None of which does us much good at the moment," said Kovac morosely, pointing to the autopilot, where a message had flashed into life. The Voyager had commenced its deceleration, and their ship's computer, obedient to its instructions, had done the same, maintaining a constant distance between the two ships.

"What do we do now, sir?" asked Villa. His tone was unimpeachably respectful, but his unspoken qualifier *if anything* could not have been clearer.

The real question, thought Rogers, *is "What can we do?" Villa obviously thinks the answer is "Nothing, with this unarmed little toy of a ship," and that the time has come for us to turn around and get the hell back to Tau Ceti with the intelligence information now in our possession.*

And let Stark and Malani get away...

Still, it's hard to argue the point. This is our last chance to break off pursuit. They've started shedding their pseudovelocity, preparatory to cutting off their drive...

All at once, an idea seemed to explode in his brain.

After a moment, the others became aware that he was sitting in preoccupied silence. At first, no one was inclined to disturb him.

"Bob," Grey finally ventured, "what is it?"

Instead of answering her, he swung toward Logan and spoke in a tightly controlled voice. "Pat, check the sensor readouts and tell me how far out that planet's Primary Limit is, relative to the Gharnakh habitat."

Logan looked puzzled, but complied. "There are the figures," he said, pointing to a screen. "As you can see, the Primary Limit is very distant, as you'd expect from that planet's monstrous gravity. And the habitat, like all the others, is orbiting well inside it."

"Makes sense," said Rogers, more to himself than to Logan. "In addition to using the planet as a gravitational anchor for their habitats, the Gharnakh'sha are also taking advantage of the friction created by its tidal forces, to give some extra heat and effectively extend the liquid-water zone. For that, they need to be in a fairly tight orbit around it." Abruptly, his voice lost its pensive tone, and he spoke crisply. "Let's get into vac suits.

We'll do it in shifts: Pat, you and your men go first, while I keep watch, then you take over for me while Grey and I do it."

Everyone looked mystified, but no one questioned what was clearly meant as an order. Logan and the two security men went aft, while Rogers watched the readouts in silence. Grey cocked her head and eyed him curiously.

"You're up to something," she stated rather than asked. "I don't suppose you're going to tell me what it is."

"Not yet—not until I've worked out all the details in my own mind." And Rogers again withdrew into intensely thoughtful silence.

Logan and the others returned, suited up, and Rogers and Grey proceeded to the locker where sufficient light-duty vac suits were kept for the Rover's full authorized complement of crew and passengers. It didn't require a very large locker, as each suit weighed only three pounds. There was no need for the things to be individually fitted; the "living" nanofabric of which they were made automatically reconfigured itself to fit any body within the normal human somatic range as a kind of skintight silvery-gray jumpsuit. They had many of the same capabilities as the Marines' light infantry field suits, but lacked the rigid armor inserts and were specialized as civilian space-survival suits. A flexible, transparent nanoplastic helmet could be readily pulled forward from a pouch behind the neck to cover the head. A small belt pack held enough highly concentrated air to pressurize the suit and provide initial life support. The "skin" was self-sealing and self-repairing; it absorbed sunlight, recycled waste, and exhaled carbon dioxide, affording an extended air and water supply. A utility belt had attachments which could be reconfigured to hold a variety of devices—including, Rogers thought, the security men's sidearms.

Finally, a small integral backpack held a grav-repulsion unit that could provide weak propulsion for extra-vehicular activity in orbital space as long as it had a gravity field of at least 0.1 g to work with. This, coincidentally, corresponded to a planet's Primary Limit—something Rogers was counting on.

They returned to the bridge, where Logan was at the controls—not that he had anything to do except observe, as the Rover's brain continued to match their quarry's deceleration. Instead of relieving him, Rogers spoke quietly.

"Now, Pat, listen carefully. When I give you the signal—which will be at a point just before the Voyager finishes reducing its pseudovelocity to zero—you will resume acceleration. Not maximum acceleration, but enough to catch up with them just after they disengage their Bernheim Drive."

For an instant, everyone stared at him as though not fully crediting what they had heard.

"But," spluttered Logan, "that means we'll be entering the giant planet's Primary Limit without having shed our pseudovelocity! Our drive will probably be wrecked!"

"That's an undeniable possibility," said Rogers calmly. "But maybe not. Remember, they'll be cutting off their drive slightly outside the Primary Limit, as per standard safety doctrine. Of course," he continued in the same deliberate tone, "we'll be cutting ours off immediately after that—another chance of damaging it. But we'll have decelerated almost to zero before the final surge of acceleration. Hopefully, by pouring on maximum deceleration after that, we'll be able to kill our pseudovelocity first."

A moment passed before anyone regained the power of speech.

"Sir," said Villa, in a stiff tone usually foreign to him, "I request permission to speak."

"Granted."

"Commander, as I understand it, you are proposing to risk passing the Primary Limit under Bernheim Drive, and then risk disengaging that drive without having succeeded in canceling the ship's pseudovelocity. Each of these things involves a significant risk of disabling the drive—perhaps beyond repair. By doing both, we will be doubling that risk." Villa paused, took a deep breath, then resumed, armored in formality. "It is hardly necessary to point out that if our Bernheim Drive is rendered inoperable, we will be stranded in this system."

"Maybe . . . but maybe not, if my plan works."

"And as to this 'plan'?" Grey inquired rather archly.

Rogers explained. Their eyes grew steadily wider as he spoke.

CHAPTER TWENTY-SIX

THE SUPERJOVIAN PLANET WAXED IN THE VIEW-FORWARD, GROW-
ing from a bright pinpoint of orange light to a perceptible disk,
as they followed the Voyager inward, matching its deceleration.

The others, who now knew Rogers' intentions, still hadn't
entirely recovered their mental equilibrium. But everyone gave
every indication of readiness. They had distributed the two security men's handguns—the only weapons aboard—with Villa and
Kovac retaining the Gauss needlers and Rogers and Grey taking
the stunners. Logan would man the piloting station. Rogers was,
as usual, less than entirely comfortable with that. But he had no
alternative, for it was out of the question that he himself should
not personally lead the desperate endeavor he had conceived.

"Here are the updated figures," said Logan tensely. "As you
see, their deceleration will kill their pseudovelocity somewhat
short of the planet's Primary Limit. Farther away from it than
we'd normally do it, in fact."

"Right," Rogers nodded, trying to seem less relieved than he
was. This was one of the things—altogether too many things—he
was counting on. "Evidently, Gharnakh pilots observe the same
kind of safety protocols ours do, only they're even more cautious."

Grey muttered something under her breath about the incon-
gruity of the words "safety" and "cautious," coming from Rogers
under the present circumstances.

Ignoring her, Rogers ran his eyes over the group one last time. "All right," he said to Villa and Kovac, "you two may as well go ahead."

"Right, Commander," they mumbled in unison, and filed into the airlock. It would only comfortably accommodate two, and Rogers wanted to have the pair already positioned in it, so as to expedite things later.

Time seemed to slow down to an agonizing crawl, as the banded gas-giant planet continued to swell. But in fact it wasn't long before Rogers, studying the unfolding figures closely, said in a tight voice, "It won't be long now, Pat."

"I know." Logan had also been watching the screen, and his voice held a slight edge of annoyance. Rogers decided to shut up and let the younger man do his job.

The two ships continued to decelerate together. By the time the Voyager had brought its pseudovelocity to zero, they had done the same. At that point, however, they ceased abruptly to imitate their quarry's movements. The Voyager, as expected, shut down its Bernheim Drive preparatory to entering the Primary Limit and proceeding planetward under photon thrusters. But at that instant, Logan applied half of the Rover's two hundred gees of acceleration, and it surged forward.

Under that powerful though insensible thrust, they soon overtook the now essentially motionless Voyager. As they neared it, and reached a point predetermined by the computer, Logan halted, abruptly reversed the Bernheim Drive's sublight thrust, and poured on a full two hundred gees of deceleration, seeking to bring them to what passed for a screeching halt at the moment they drew abreast of the other ship. Rogers continued to keep quiet, with an effort, and contented himself with offering up a silent prayer to any gods that might ever have existed that the Gharnakh pilot wouldn't reactivate his drive and throw their calculations into limbo.

The Gharnakh'sha didn't, possibly because he flinched from doing so this close to the Primary Limit and possibly because he was stunned into immobility by this new turn of events. But Rogers' calculations had, he now realized, been cut too close from the first. He saw that their pseudovelocity would not quite be cancelled out before they overshot their prey.

"Kill the drive!" he snapped. "*Now!*"

Logan didn't hesitate, even though he was being ordered to throw his piloting training to the winds. He instantly deactivated the Bernheim Drive in the midst of its furious deceleration. The inertial compensators prevented them from being thrown to the deck as the Rover came to an instantaneous halt. But from the engineering spaces aft came the dull sound of a kind of soft explosion, and their noses twitched to the smell of an acrid vapor.

Rogers paid no attention to any of it. There would—if all went according to plan—be time to inspect the drive later. All that mattered at the moment was that his instinct had been correct: The Voyager lay off to port, even closer than he had hoped, motionless relative to their ship since both retained the same intrinsic actual vector from Tau Ceti.

As he watched, the light-cone of the Voyager's photon thruster appeared and it began to draw slowly ahead. But Logan, as per instructions, immediately followed suit.

"Tractor beam!" Rogers rasped, while thinking a silent apology for ever having doubted Logan as a pilot.

The remote-focused gravitic effect known as a tractor beam was mounted by most spacecraft, if only as a cargo-handling tool. It had little application in space combat because warships were routinely equipped with "shears," specialized versions exerting an interference force which, when targeted on a tractor beam, broke its grip. But civilian craft never carried shears, having no need of them. Stark's Voyager was no exception. So, when Logan slapped a tractor beam on it, set at a force calculated to hold it just so close but no closer, the two ships were locked into a single rigid unit. Logan then cut out his photon thrusters, leaving those of the quarry—relatively feeble, intended only for orbital maneuvering within a Primary Limit and atmospheric flight with the aid of grav repulsion—to move the added mass of the Rover as well as its own, so its acceleration grew sluggish indeed. And even as Rogers watched the readouts, they passed within the Primary Limit, so safe reactivation of the Voyager's Bernheim Drive was impossible.

"Go!" ordered Rogers into the tiny communicator in his vac suit's helmet. Villa and Kovac obeyed, and Rogers heard the sound of the airlock opening and closing.

"All right, Grey. Let's go. Pat," Rogers added unnecessarily, "stay alert for anything." He and Grey sprinted for the airlock.

He had tried to order her to remain aboard the Rover, but she had insisted that her duty as a New American law enforcement officer mandated her direct participation, given Stark's crimes. Rogers had suspected that her motivation wasn't entirely official, but he had yielded on the point. And, in truth, his heart had never really been in his attempt to exclude her. He wanted her along—a feeling he rationalized by telling himself that she was good with weapons. Also, she was not entirely without experience of extra-vehicular activity, having been involved in some anti-smuggling operations in orbital space.

They crowded into the airlock and Rogers hastily cycled them through. Expelled by the escaping air, they emerged into the light of the orange-and-yellow-banded giant planet, several of whose small moons were now naked-eye objects, as was the ring habitat off to the side. But Rogers had no eyes for the scenery. He spotted the two security men, nearing a rendezvous with the Voyager. He and Grey followed, at an angle calculated to compensate for the slow acceleration of the two gravitationally linked ships, lest they be left behind in the void. Barely inside the Primary Limit as they were, their backpack grav-repulsion units had just enough of a gravity field to leverage. But, straining, they closed the gap.

As they neared the Voyager, Rogers wondered with a grim smile what its occupants were thinking. They must, he thought, be stewing over their inability to do anything, for their craft was as unarmed as the Rover and was held in the gravitic grip of its tractor beam.

Ahead, Rogers saw Villa and Kovac reach the Voyager's side and stand on it, held in place by the magnetized soles that were a feature of the light-duty vac suits. The two began to walk slowly and carefully toward the passenger airlock. Then Rogers and Grey commenced the rather awkward maneuvering required for a feet-first approach. Presently, they felt the soft clamping sensation, almost like suction, as the magnetism took hold. Very gingerly, they moved to join the other two, who by now had reached the airlock. Kovac was already at work.

Spacecraft designers had always recognized that contingencies might arise in which all of a vessel's occupants were unconscious or incapacitated and rescuers needed to open its airlock from the outside without help from the inside. Less publicly emphasized was the thought that law enforcers might have occasion to require access to uncooperative ships. All airlocks were designed accordingly, although military ships (which the Voyager was not) possessed an override feature by which they could prevent uninvited ingress. Special training was required to thus gain unassisted entry; emergency responders of all sorts received that training... including security personnel like Kovac.

As he waited, Rogers sweated. So far, all the suppositions he had been relying on had proven correct. But the removal of those worries merely made room for new ones. He had no idea how many men Stark and Malani had with them, but it couldn't be too many; the Voyager wasn't tremendously more capacious than their own Rover. By the same token, he was confident that the hostages—who were no longer needed, as far as their captors knew, and for whom there would be no room—had been left behind at the Gharnakh station in the Tau Ceti system, which meant that the leadership of the Sons of Arnold were either dead or in custody by now. But his final assumption was a good deal shakier: that the terrorists would not be armed heavily, if at all. It seemed reasonable—what need was there for weapons among friends, aboard one's own ship?—but he was uneasily aware that he was not dealing with reasonable people.

Kovac finished his manipulations. The outer door of the airlock opened. They all crowded in before it closed—this was a roomier airlock than the Rover's—and hastily pulled back their flexible helmets as air filled the chamber and the inner door slid aside.

They had discussed and planned their next move to the point where there need be no hesitation. Rogers' original idea had been for Kovac and Villa to instantly spray the interior with a fusillade of flechettes from their Gauss pistols. But Grey, while admitting the validity of his reasoning concerning the probable absence of hostages, had argued against the use of random lethal force, given their lack of absolute certainty. Thus it was that she and Rogers, without exposing themselves unnecessarily, swung their stunners from side to side, unaimed, unleashing a rapid-fire series of discharges that would hopefully render anyone standing around the airlock unconscious. Then they stood aside and the two security men plunged through into the main cabin, Gauss pistols at the ready. Rogers and Grey immediately followed them.

The scene that met their eyes confirmed that Stark's hostages were not there. Otherwise, it was the last thing Rogers would have expected.

Two bodies lay sprawled on the deck. Both, judging from their ethnic features, were Sons of Wilkinson. And neither was merely stunned. Both were quite dead, judging from the pools of blood slowly spreading away from their cut throats.

Farther back, two others of apparent New American ancestry—one of whom was Ethan Stark—were being held in the grips of Near Eastern–looking captors so as to serve as human shields, with knives to their throats. *Knives,* flashed through Rogers' mind. *Of course they'd have those.*

Khalid al-Malani also had a knife. He stood sheltering behind the others, eyes blazing with fanaticism. In the background, Rogers saw that this ship had a raised, open bridge not unlike that of the Rover. There, a Gharnakh'sha lay sprawled, motionless and, Rogers was certain, dead. One of Malani's men crouched over the nonhuman body, using it as a shield as he lowered himself into the pilot's chair from which the alien had slumped. He held a knife stained with the yellowish maroon-colored fluid the Gharnakh'sha used for blood.

"Leave, or we will kill these two," said Malani. His voice was a croon, as though he was in the grip of a veritable ecstasy of hate. "Of course you care nothing for the lives of the faithful. But because these are fellow infidels, perhaps you think their lives are not worthless."

CHAPTER TWENTY-SEVEN

ROGERS POINTED TO THE DEAD GHARNAKH PILOT. "AREN'T YOUR Gharnakh friends going to be a little upset about that, even if we do let you go?" he asked, playing for time as he hastily assessed the situation. He saw at once that neither he nor his companions could get a clear shot at Malani or his henchmen, who were bunched tightly behind their two captives. And his stun pistol had a very limited range; he doubted it would reach the man on the bridge. Villa or Kovac, he was confident, could put a flechette into that man, but it was less certain that that flechette would go all the way through the thick, dense alien body he was sheltering behind.

"We'll blame it on you," said Malani, with a self-satisfied smirk. "They're expecting us—a courier boat came here before we left Tau Ceti, letting them know we were coming."

"Be that as it may, what gives you the idea that we give a damn about the lives of these two?" Rogers gestured contemptuously at the two Sons of Wilkinson—although, in truth, he preferred to take Stark alive for interrogation. As he did so, he spared a side-glance for Grey. Her eyes were locked with Stark's. And unless Rogers was mistaken, there was an unmistakable ambivalence in her expression.

"Then maybe you'll care about *this*!" cried Malani before

Rogers could worry about what he thought he was seeing in Grey. He jerked his chin in the direction of the man crouched at the piloting station. "You see Tariq, up there? He has some piloting training. Unless you leave and allow us to proceed to the Gharnakh habitat, we'll apply a lateral thrust with this ship's Bernheim Drive, and at the same time use its tractor beam to draw it into a collision with your ship. He's already set the controls, so even if you decide to go ahead and kill your two fellow *Feringhi* to get us, there's nothing you'll be able to do about it!"

"Spare me your bluffs," said Rogers, keeping his voice level. "You can't activate your Bernheim Drive. We're well inside the planet's Primary Limit by now." And with some fraction of his consciousness, he saw in the bridge viewscreen that the ring habitat was now quite visible as a tiny circle with a point of light at its center, as they drew closer to it perpendicular to its plane of rotation.

"The drive won't need to last for more than a few seconds, nor will it have to operate at full efficiency," Malani declared. "At this distance, that's all it will take. And even if whoever is piloting your ship disengages his tractor beam, ours will make it impossible for him to get away."

"And we'll all die—you as well as us. You have, I assume, considered that?"

"Yes! *Shaitan* will seize the souls of you pork-eating dogs of unbelievers, while my men and I go directly to paradise!"

"But I notice you're using the threat of that to talk us into simply leaving and letting you go," Rogers observed insouciantly. "It seems you're not quite ready to get started on your seventy virgins yet."

Malani looked ready to ignite with white-hot hate.

"He means it," Stark choked out, his larynx constricted as he flinched from the curved dagger at his throat. "For God's sake, do as he says!" His eyes pleaded, and were distended with terror. Rogers lost whatever limited respect he'd had for him as a villain.

Suddenly, Grey seemed to convulse with emotion. "Oh, Ethan," she cried, her voice almost a sob. Before anyone was aware of what was happening, she flung herself forward, dropping her stun pistol to the deck as she went to her knees at Stark's feet and embraced him around the waist. "Ethan, I'm so sorry! It's because of me that it's come to this. They can't do this to you!"

For the moment, everyone stood paralyzed with startlement—including the man holding Stark, who looked down, clearly bewildered by this unexpected turn of events. His knife-hand wavered slightly.

In mid-sob, Grey reached down with her right hand, scooped up the stunner she had dropped, brought it up in a smooth, quick motion to the side of the Caliphate man, and pressed the firing stud. At the same instant that he went rigid and then limp, she reached up with her left hand, grabbed the wrist of his knife-arm as it involuntarily spasmed, and forced it away from Stark's throat before the knife-edge could make more than a small, shallow incision. The man crumpled forward, with Grey and Stark beneath him. With their cluster broken up, the Caliphate men were exposed.

Instantly, the shocked tableau exploded into pandemonium.

The man holding the other Son of Wilkinson was, by some small fraction of a second, the first to react. He drew his knife across the throat of his captive, who tried to scream but only produced a gurgle of blood. At appreciably the same moment, Kovac ripped both of them open with a quick burst of flechettes. Rogers forcibly shook off the whipsawlike emotional effects of Grey's succession of actions; he stunned Malani, who, now fully exposed, was drawing back his dagger as though to throw it. Simultaneously, Villa sprang forward, his Gauss pistol on full automatic, sending a steady stream of flechettes into and around the dead Gharnakh'sha on the bridge. Tariq's head bobbed momentarily above the alien carcass, and one of the high-velocity steel slivers went through it. It didn't blow out the top of the cranium in a shower of blood and gray matter as a heavy slug would have; but, passing through the brain, it was just as lethal in its own less spectacularly sanguinary way.

Leaping over Malani's unconscious form, Rogers ran through the cabin and bounded up to the bridge. With frantic haste, he hauled the two corpses, of as many different species, off the piloting station and ran his eyes over the controls. Almost weak with relief, he saw that Tariq hadn't had time to engage the Bernheim Drive. He had, however, attached a tractor beam to the Rover. With a poorly aimed slap at the control board, Rogers cut it off. He then performed the slightly more complex operation of deactivating the photon thrusters, and the two linked craft continued on course in free fall. Only then did he turn to the comm console.

"Pat, this is Rogers. Acknowledge!"

"Acknowledging, Commander," came the Australian twang. "What's happening over there? For a moment, this ship was being tractored at full power, but then the beam cut off before we were pulled together very much. And—"

"Details later. We've secured this ship, and I've shut down its photon thrusters. So you can turn things over to the autopilot and go assess the damage to our Bernheim Drive."

"Right." A moment passed. "Done—we're on autopilot and are continuing on our present trajectory. Uh...Commander, do you expect that the Gharnakh'sha are going to take any action?"

Rogers had been thinking the same thing...and now he glanced at the viewscreen, where the ring of the Gharnakh habitat was disobligingly becoming more visible. "Maybe not at once. Malani mentioned that they're expected, so as long as we stay on course we probably have a little time before they begin to get suspicious. But not much time. Get busy and inspect the drive."

"Right, sir. Signing off."

Rogers strode back down into the cabin. Kovac and Villa had bound Malani in strips torn from his own clothing. Now they were doing the same to the other surviving Caliphate man, allowing Grey and Stark to get to their feet from beneath him.

"Grey," said Stark with a glowing smile, "I always knew you'd—"

"You're under arrest," she cut in coolly. And, with a total absence of expression, she brought up her sidearm and stunned him. As he collapsed to the deck, she turned to Rogers with a look that said everything should now stand as explained.

And yet he couldn't forget the urgency with which she had forced the spasming knife-hand away from Stark's throat.

CHAPTER TWENTY-EIGHT

"AND THAT'S THE STORY, COMMANDER," LOGAN FINISHED HIS report. "The strain of deactivating it before shedding all the pseudovelocity was too much for the Bernheim Drive. It may not be a total loss, but repairing it is probably a job for a shipyard. Even if we could do it ourselves, which I doubt, it would take—"

"Longer than we've got," Rogers finished for him. "Anyway, we don't need it. All right, Pat. You've done all you can. Use your tractor beam and your maneuvering thrusters to bring yourself alongside, seal your airlock to ours, and come aboard."

Signing off, he looked around him and became aware of the other three close behind him. They had cleaned up as much of the mess as possible, ejected the bodies out the airlock, and confined Stark, Malani and Malani's surviving goon, bound and gagged, in a cargo compartment where they could await the unpleasant sensation of regaining consciousness. Now they had crowded in around the piloting station.

"Well," said Grey in a tone that hovered ambiguously between accusation and grudging approval, "now I see why you were willing to risk wrecking the Rover's Bernheim Drive. You were counting on being able to help yourself to this ship."

"You've grasped it." Rogers permitted himself a heartbeat of self-satisfaction before glumness settled back over him.

"Of course, if they had wrecked *their* drive, we'd be stuck in this system," she pointed out. "You were lucky."

"You'd better hope I continue to be," he said grimly, indicating the viewscreen and the readouts.

Dead ahead, the ring habitat was continuing to wax, with the great banded sphere of the superjovian planet off to the right, the faint ring common to practically all gas giants now visible. They were now close enough for the sensors to have picked up more details on the habitat—including the fact that it was not defenseless. Its outer surface was studded with what had to be laser-weapon emplacements—quite heavy ones, to be recognizable as such at this range. However, there was no warship activity around it. Clearly, although not undefended, it was not a naval installation.

Nevertheless, there *was* a Gharnakh naval installation in orbit around the mammoth planet, perhaps on one of its small moons in a lower orbit, for a pair of ships had appeared, coming around from behind the planet off to the right. Although they were too distant for any details to have emerged, the computer inferred from the sensor readings that they were roughly equivalent to Imperial fifth-raters. Another computer deduction was that their photon rockets produced no more gees of acceleration than those of the Voyager. But then, neither did those of an Imperial warship; there was no need, as they were intended only for maneuvering within a Primary Limit. And these ships' thrusters were moving them into an orbit that was unmistakably an intercept course.

Logan had joined them, and he watched those two red icons in the astrogation plot intently. "It would seem that the safety margin you said we had has expired," he said drily.

"Yes," Rogers admitted. "Not too surprising. Eventually they were bound to conclude that there was something suspicious about our approach. There have been a couple of attempts to contact us. I haven't answered; I considered trying to pretend I was Stark, but they would have wanted to talk to the Gharnakh pilot."

"The good news," said Logan, "is that it will take them a while to intercept us, here within the Primary Limit using reaction drives."

"Bob," said Grey, sounding slightly puzzled, "shouldn't we be, uh, turning around and getting away?"

Rogers smiled, briefly and humorlessly. "Like all of us, you're spoiled by the capabilities of the Bernheim Drive in slower-than-light mode. It produces such tremendous accelerations that we can do maneuvers beyond the dreams of the early space pioneers. But *only* outside a Primary Limit. Inside it, we're back to where they were then, almost three hundred years ago, limited to reaction drives. Oh, of course our photon thrusters are far better than anything they had in those days—ion drives, fission rockets and, God help them, chemical rockets. But they're still, fundamentally, reaction drives, and they only produce a couple of gees of acceleration. Essentially, we're as much at the mercy of the local gravity field as sailing ships were at the mercy of the winds and currents."

"But," she persisted, "if we can get outside the Primary Limit, we can use the Bernheim Drive."

"So can they," Rogers reminded her. "And those are warships. If their design philosophies were anything like those of Imperial combatant ships, their Bernheim Drives are a lot more powerful than this ship's—maybe twice as much so."

"But as I understand it, if we pass the local star's Secondary Limit and go faster-than-light, we'll be invulnerable to their weapons."

Rogers shook his head. "I don't even need to run the problem through the computer to know the answer. Even assuming that we got beyond the Primary Limit before they did, they could overhaul us before we reach the Secondary Limit. And ships in slower-than-light mode *can* exchange fire." *Not that it would exactly be an "exchange" in this case,* he thought mordantly.

"And as far as I can see," said Logan, sounding as morose as Rogers felt, "we can't even beat them past the Primary Limit. We're still being drawn in toward the habitat by that planet's gravity."

Rogers nodded, looking at the figures. They were still gaining velocity, under the pull of the monster planet's terrific gravitation...

All at once, the solution came to him.

In a fury of wordless intensity, he turned to the astrogation computer and began punching in numbers. The others looked at him, puzzled.

"Commander—?" Villa began.

"Quiet!" snapped Rogers with unintended harshness. "Leave me alone. I have to find out if something is possible."

They all held their peace for a few minutes while he worked

in silence. Then he sat back with a sigh of relief and turned to face them.

"The problem can be stated as follows," he began. "We need to get beyond the Primary Limit so far ahead of them that our Bernheim Drive, going slower-than-light, can get us to the Secondary Limit before they can catch us. There's only one way we have a chance of doing that. We have to use something nobody has had occasion to use ever since the Bernheim Drive was invented: the gravitational slingshot effect."

Logan's brow furrowed. "I seem to remember reading about that—a technique they used in the early days of interplanetary flight. But I don't recall the details."

Rogers turned back to the computer and punched controls, and a holographic display appeared. It showed the planet as an orange sphere, a purple icon representing the Gharnakh habitat, and their own location and course. "Instead of fighting this planet's gravity, we'll put it to work for us. We'll fall inward, toward the limb of the planet." He touched the controls again, and the computer projected their course ahead in a line of glowing dots. "By the time we reach that point, we will have reached a tremendous velocity. Then, at that precise point—and it has to be very precise—we use our photon thrusters to break us loose so we're flung outward at that velocity."

"Can't the Gharnakh ships do the same thing?" asked Kovac, who seemed to be having difficulty following this.

"No, because unlike us they aren't being pulled in toward the planet; they're in orbit around it, and starting from a lower orbit. They'll have to struggle up out of the gravity well."

"But Bob," said Grey, "will this give us enough of a head start to pass the Secondary Limit ahead of them?"

Rogers slumped a bit. "There you have me. I lack the crucial variable: the strength of those ships' Bernheim Drives. If their designs are maximized for speed, the answer to your question is, I'm afraid, 'Almost.' But if they're balanced designs, trading some speed for weapons and defenses, we ought to be able to make it. And at any rate," he finished, looking around at all of them, "does anybody have any other suggestions?"

No one did.

"Just one problem you haven't mentioned, sir," said Villa, carefully respectful. He pointed to the line of glowing dots. It touched the purple icon. "This projected course will bring us very close to the Gharnakh ring habitat."

"That's right," said Kovac, back on familiar ground. "Those laser turrets on the outside surface will vaporize us as we go by."

Rogers grinned. "You've put your finger on the crucial point: They're on the *outside* surface." They all looked blank. He elaborated. "We're not going past the habitat. We're going *through* it!"

The inertial compensators prevented them from feeling any g-forces as the photon thrusters, blaring at full power, combined with the planet's gravitational tug to drive them toward the needle they would thread.

Actually, the habitat, growing in the view-forward at an ever-accelerating rate, resembled more and more a titanic wedding band, wider than usual and with a glowing illumination source suspended at its center. They would, of course, have to avoid that small artificial sun. But the ring had a radius of six hundred miles, so even subtracting the hundred-mile height of the atmosphere wall, they had a margin of almost five hundred miles, and theirs was a small vessel.

Still, Rogers reflected, compared to the magnitudes with which a space pilot usually dealt, this was an awfully *small* needle to thread at a velocity measured in a great many miles per second. Nor did it help that it was a *moving* needle; he would have to compensate very carefully for the habitat's orbital velocity. But, he told himself, they would flash through that three-hundred-mile width in such a brief instant that it shouldn't be much of a factor; the habitat wouldn't have time to move much.

He spared a glance for the holo-display. They had cast the Rover adrift, with its autopilot under instruction to veer off, in the hope of deceiving their pursuers. It hadn't worked. The Gharnakh warships were continuing on course, piling on their maximum acceleration. But they had been doing that already, and they were clearly straining to claw their way up from a lower orbit. Then, dismissing them from his mind, he focused his entire consciousness on the fat ring that was coming closer and closer. Soon it seemed to be hurtling toward them as though flung by a playful—or angry—god.

Rogers felt a pressure on his right shoulder: Grey's hand, squeezing hard.

He couldn't spare even a small fraction of his mind to wonder what the inhabitants of the ring were thinking. Perhaps their rulers hadn't told them anything was happening.

At the last moment, he cut off the photon thrusters.

Then, with terrible speed, the ring was all around them. Involuntarily, irrationally, they all flinched.

For little more than a heartbeat, they were within it, plunging through. The light source flashed by like a streak of lightning to the left. In that single, unimaginable instant, Rogers glimpsed the ring's inner surface. His mind barely registered the artificial landscape—gleaming lakes and rivers, corrugated hills, cities whose architecture was so titanic as to seem like natural features save for its geometrical regularity—and then they were through and away, and the ring was receding in the view-aft, dwindling with soul-shaking speed.

Rogers shook himself free of the mind-numbing moment he had just experienced, and did two things. First he checked a certain sensor. The Voyager's outer skin hadn't appreciably heated from atmospheric friction. Good. He hadn't known how much leakage there was over the atmosphere walls, but clearly there was very little, hence very few air molecules floating about within the ring. He hadn't expected any serious overheating in such a brief passage, but he might have caused cyclonic winds on the inner surface.

The second thing he did was resume acceleration with the photon thrusters.

He became aware that Grey was giving him an odd look. "Why did you stop accelerating and go through in free fall?" she asked.

"Well, I probably didn't need to. Given the margin of a few hundred miles that we had, I doubt if the exhaust cone would have caused any destruction on the inner surface. But why take chances? As it is... I don't know if the Gharnakh'sha have nervous breakdowns, but if they do there are probably a lot of them back there just now."

Her look grew even odder, and more intense. "But they're aliens—and aliens whose government is hostile to the Empire, at that. Why did you give a damn?"

He matched her look for look. "They're sentient beings. And I don't believe in random mass killing. Only fanatics do—people so obsessed with ideological abstractions that life means nothing to them. The kind of people that the Empire has prevented from ruining the world in the name of some fine-sounding ideal or other."

He expected an argument. But she only looked thoughtful.

The inertial compensators were not magic, and Rogers was unsure of how well they would be able to cope with the stresses the g-forces would inflict on them at the crucial moment. But he was taking no chances. As they fell toward their closest approach to the now unsettlingly nearby giant planet, Rogers ordered everyone to strap in—something people didn't often have to do in modern spacecraft. Logan secured himself beside him on the bridge; the others took seats in the cabin behind.

It was well that they did. It turned out to be worse than Rogers had anticipated. The ship shuddered to vibrations he was afraid would shake it apart. All of them were flung violently back and forth against their straps. Grimly, Rogers forced himself to remain focused on the instruments, awaiting the precise moment to reignite the photon rockets.

His moment of piloting instinct was true. The Voyager caromed off the planet's gravity field like a thrown pebble skipping off a pond, and headed outward by momentum as well as its reaction drive. The angry reddish sphere began to recede in the view-aft.

Logan—as thoroughly bathed in sweat as Rogers knew he himself was—was grinning. His voice was shaky but exultant. "You did it, Commander."

Rogers expelled a long sigh. "We're naturally not even close to being on course for Tau Ceti. But once we pass the planet's Primary Limit, we can use the Bernheim Drive to come around." He set the autopilot, then unstrapped. Behind him, he heard a series of clicks as the others did the same. "All right, everybody," he called out, stretching hugely. "You can—"

"FREEZE!" came a familiar voice. "Then turn around slowly, with your hands in view."

Rogers obeyed, and looked down into the cabin. Ethan Stark was aiming a Gauss pistol at them. His eyes were wild, but his gun hand was disconcertingly steady. It was easy to see where the pistol had come from. David Villa lay slumped over the side of his chair. His holster was empty. And a kind of steel sliver protruded from his right temple.

CHAPTER TWENTY-NINE

"TAKE OUT YOUR WEAPONS—*VERY* SLOWLY—AND PUT THEM DOWN," Stark rasped.

They all obeyed, knowing what a Gauss weapon on full automatic could do. Rogers and Grey dropped their stunners. Kovac, standing beside Grey, placed his needler on the deck with somewhat more care. Then Stark relaxed a trifle and favored them with a grin of mad triumph.

"Surprised, aren't you? I've always had that steel splinter in a special compartment in my shoe, just in case. The way I was tied up, I was able to get it out and use it to cut myself loose."

Kovac, who had searched and bound Stark, gave Rogers an it-won't-happen-again look.

"And then," Stark gloated on, "I used it on Malani and the other raghead. You'll find what's left of them in that compartment. By the way, thanks for confining us together in there. I was able to take my time with them while you were busy. Not as much time as I would have liked. Malani betrayed me! I was a fool to trust a slime mold like that. He died too easily. Still, I was able to make it last...make it last..." His eyes began to take on a dreamy look. But before Rogers could try to take advantage, he blinked and snapped back into focus.

"Afterwards," he resumed in a more or less normal voice,

"I had no trouble getting out; that door isn't designed to keep people in, you know. Just as I did, that god-awful vibration began. I almost lost consciousness. But then, while all of you were recovering, I was able to come up behind you unnoticed." Stark paused and looked around at them, as though expecting praise for his cleverness.

Rogers didn't oblige him. "So tell me," he said, keeping his voice level, "why haven't you killed us all?"

"Believe me, I'd love nothing better. But I'm not a pilot, Rogers. I need you."

Rogers saw no purpose to be served by revealing that Logan was also a qualified pilot. He hoped the Australian would have the sense to keep his mouth shut.

"By the way," said Stark, "what *was* that vibration, anyway? I though the ship was going to be shaken apart."

"Never mind. All you need to know is that we're now on autopilot, headed away from the planet at a high velocity, and will soon go past the Primary Limit. The Gharnakh'sha can't catch us." Rogers mentally crossed his fingers at that last, and hoped it was true.

"It doesn't matter. As soon as we're outside the Primary Limit, you can use the Bernheim Drive to turn us around. And then you'll broadcast a surrender offer to the Gharnakh'sha—they must have ships pursuing you by now, and those ships' computers will have translation programs. They'll have reason to be grateful to me for presenting them with an Imperial intelligence officer for interrogation." Stark's face turned ugly. "Enough talk! Get back to the piloting station and get ready to activate the drive."

Rogers appeared to consider. "Actually, I don't believe I'll do any of these things."

Stark's face quivered with rage. "Do as I say, damn you! Or I'll—"

"You'll what? Kill me? Then where will you be, without a pilot?" To Rogers' relief, Logan held his peace.

"Kill you?" Stark took on a look of psychotic craft. "No. But I can kill these others if you don't obey me. Why do you think I've let them live this long? So you see, their lives are in your hands. It won't be my fault if they die!" He turned to Grey, and his expression grew especially ugly. "First of all, I'll kill this bitch. In fact, I may kill her anyway and keep the other two as hostages for your good behavior. She betrayed our cause. She betrayed *me*! Everyone betrays me!" He was almost frothing now. "And before I kill her I'll—"

"Oh, Ethan," Grey blurted, "can't you *see*? I didn't betray you—I saved your life. I had to do what I did. It was the only way to keep that man with the knife to your throat from killing you."

For an instant, Stark's face went slack. Then it twisted into a snarl. "Do you think you can trick me again? How stupid do you think I am? Right afterwards, you stunned me!"

"Don't you understand? I had to do that in order keep *him* thinking I had abandoned our cause." She jerked her chin scornfully in Rogers' direction. "But I never have. I've just been leading him on."

At the core of Rogers' being was a dead lump.

Stark's resolve visibly wavered, although his gun hand did not. "How can I trust you, after all that's happened?"

"I tell you, it's all been to fool him! I've never stopped loving you. And now I'll join you here, in exile among the Gharnakh'sha. Together, we'll be able to pool our knowledge of history to help the Gharnakh'sha plan their time-travel expedition. We can tell them precisely which targets to select."

Something like joy awoke in Stark's eyes, at the mention of the Gharnakh lie which he had accepted so avidly, and on which he had built cloud-castles of hope. "What? You mean you know that's true?"

"Of course, Ethan. I've believed it all along. *You* said it, so it must be true! I was just pretending to doubt it, in Rogers' hearing. I want to be part of turning such a beautiful dream into reality. But most importantly, we'll be together."

For the first time, Stark's eyes lost their focus, and he unsteadily lowered his needler.

Too abruptly for the action even to be startling, Grey dropped to the deck, rolled, and grabbed Kovac's needler.

With an inarticulate howl, Stark unleased a burst of flechettes. Impacting the deck at an angle, they ricocheted wildly around the cabin. Rogers, Logan and Kovac went prone to avoid the shower of death. Grey continued rolling, but not quite fast enough. A flechette ripped into her upper left arm. She screamed, but at the same instant she completed her roll, ending on her back, and brought up the needler, firing on autoburst as she raised it. The stream of flechettes first tore into Stark's groin, then stitched a line of holes up his torso. One of them went through his heart, releasing a spray of blood. He opened his mouth, but only a flow of blood emerged from it. He crumpled to the deck.

Kovac was already on his knees beside Grey, tearing off a strip of clothing to use as a bandage, when Rogers and Logan bounded down from the bridge. Logan ran to the starboard bulkhead for the first aid kit. Rogers knelt beside Grey, and their eyes met. No words were needed.

"Well," he said, a little too briskly, "I'd better get back to the piloting station. We'll be reaching the Primary Limit very soon."

The Gharnakh ships passed the Primary Limit a little closer behind them than Rogers had counted on. But their Bernheim Drives turned out to produce somewhat less sublight acceleration than those of Imperial warships of comparable tonnage. And, not being capital ships, they were too small to carry the big Bernheim Drive-powered torpedoes. So it was only necessary to reach Chi Eridani A's Secondary Limit before those ships could close within beam-weapon range.

One hell of an "only," Rogers mentally groused as he watched their pursuers draw inexorably closer and closer. But the computer assured him that they would make it—assuming that he ignored the usual safety margin and formed the warp field when they were just barely outside the Secondary Limit.

In the end, he cut it finer than he liked—neither he nor Logan burdened the other two with the knowledge of just how fine. But the computer had not lied. When they went into a bubble in space-time where no weapons could touch them, everyone was too relieved even to raise a cheer.

"Well, that's that," sighed Rogers. "Next stop, Tau Ceti." He decided it would be in questionable taste to mention that they had an ample supply of food, inasmuch as its ampleness was accounted for by the deaths of four people, including that of Villa, whose body they had put into deep freeze for honorable burial. He also decided against mentioning the complexities that awaited them when it became necessary to account for Grey's role, or roles. *Plenty of time to worry about that later,* he thought.

"I suppose those Gharnakh ships have turned back for home by now," said Grey after a while. "They could catch up to us pretty easily, but they know it wouldn't do any good."

"They must be gnashing their teeth, or whatever it is they do," Kovac chuckled.

"I'm afraid not." The flat voice was that of Logan, who had been standing watch at the piloting station. The other three exchanged a quick, anxious glance and crowded up onto the bridge. Logan pointed to the sensor display. Two ships were now ahead of them so the passive sensors could detect them... but presumably not for long, because they were moving farther and farther ahead under the power of their military-grade drives, leaving the Voyager behind, and would soon be out of sensor range.

"They didn't turn back," said Rogers unnecessarily. "They're more determined to catch us than we thought. They followed us past the Secondary Limit and went faster-than-light."

"But *why*?" demanded Kovac, scowling. "It's like Grey said: They can't hurt us."

"I think I know why," said Rogers. "At first they stayed behind, where they could detect us but we couldn't detect them. This enabled them to determine our course—or, I should say, confirm it, since they must have known we'd be headed for Tau Ceti. And now they've gone to full power and will reach Tau Ceti before we do... and be ready for us when we go slower-than-light."

An uncomfortable silence ensued.

"But," said Kovac, in a hopeful tone, "they don't know just exactly where, in the Tau Ceti system, we'll appear."

Rogers turned to the computer and brought up a holo-display of Tau Ceti. "They know we'll have to shut down the warp field before we enter the Secondary Limit. Of course, there's no reason why we have to wait that long. I suppose we could head toward Washington Station instead of New America—"

"Or maybe some random point," Grey ventured.

"I don't think that will do any good," said Logan bleakly. "I think what they plan to do is kill their warp fields somewhere outside Tau Ceti's Secondary Limit and lie in wait. As soon as we go slower-than-light, they'll just do a faster-than-light hop and be on top of us just before we get inside the Secondary Limit. After that, it won't take them long to catch us."

"I think you're right," said Rogers heavily.

If possible, the silence was more profound than before. After a moment, Grey broke it.

"I think the solution is obvious."

"To you, maybe," muttered Kovac.

"Let's hear it," urged Rogers.

"I say, let's not go to Tau Ceti at all. Instead, we change course—now that they can't detect us—and go straight to Sol. They'll be left sitting in the outskirts of the Tau Ceti system, looking stupid."

At first, all the others could do was stare at her.

"We'd be going there eventually anyway," she continued. "It's vital that the information in our possession gets to the Empire."

"To the *Empire*?" Rogers looked at her appraisingly. "That's the last thing I would have expected to hear you say. Is it possible that you've decided that, historically, things turned out for the best after all?"

"Not exactly." She frowned as though seeking to sort out her own thoughts. "I still think things could have come out better in the eighteenth century—that there could have been a better outcome to the First North American Rebellion. The passage of time doesn't make a wrong right, but beyond a certain point it creates a situation where the wrong can't be righted without inflicting even greater wrongs." She sighed. "No. After a while we just have to accept what history has offered us and make the most of it."

Rogers cocked his head and favored her with a crooked smile. "Even when I'm a part of what history has offered you?"

She smiled back. "Even then."

And so it was settled. Rogers altered their heading, toward their as-yet-invisible goal. Then, after setting in the new course, he leaned back in the pilot's chair. Grey was seated beside him.

"Naturally," he drawled, "it would *never* occur to me to think that your suggestion had any ulterior motive—like putting off the day when we have to see about salvaging your NAISA career."

"'We'?" she queried.

"Yes," he said, suddenly serious. "I intend to be there with you."

"Somehow, I believe you. Even though by now I ought to know better."

"You know," he began after a moment, "I have a feeling we may have gotten off on the wrong foot—"

"I seem to recall you saying that once before," she said archly.

Rogers had the grace to look abashed. But she didn't follow up on her advantage.

After a moment, he cleared his throat. "Uh... there is, of course, no privacy aboard this boat..." Then he became aware that Logan and Villa were standing close behind them. Both were grinning.

"We ought to be able to organize something," said Logan, his grin widening.

After a time that seemed shorter than it was, Sol became a naked-eye object, gleaming far ahead.

‖‖‖‖‖‖‖‖‖‖‖‖‖‖‖‖‖‖‖‖‖‖‖‖‖‖‖‖‖‖
AUTHOR'S NOTE
‖‖‖‖‖‖‖‖‖‖‖‖‖‖‖‖‖‖‖‖‖‖‖‖‖‖‖‖‖‖‖‖

COULD THE AMERICAN REVOLUTION HAVE BEEN AVOIDED? AN excellent case can be made (and, in fact, *has* been made by Caleb Carr in *What Ifs of American History,* edited by Robert Crowley) that it could very well have been averted on a basis of imperial reform and reorganization had William Pitt the Elder been in a better position to exercise political leadership in the years following the repeal of the Stamp Act in 1766. But could it have been patched up on the same basis after the Declaration of Independence had been signed and fighting had already commenced, as I have postulated? This is a good deal more problematical, which is why I have tinkered with dynastic history to provide Britain with a more sensible king than George III during the crucial period.

All of which, of course, begs the question of whether it *should* have been patched up. Honesty compels me to admit that I have days when I think the smart move for my American ancestors would have been to stay in the British Empire, which after another century or so would have been effectively an American empire. And, just incidentally, slavery would have ended a generation earlier, without a four-year bloodbath of a war. (It was abolished throughout the British Empire in 1833; and the Southern slaveholders, who in our timeline went into rebellion in the firm—though, as it turned out, mistaken—belief that they could count on British help, would never have been insane enough to try it *knowing* that they would have to face the equivalent of actual history's northern states and British Empire combined.) Under these circumstances, I think it not unreasonable to suppose that the idea of "Imperial Federation" championed in the late nineteenth century by the likes of John Robert Seeley, J. A. Froude and Joseph Chamberlain (sometimes called "Greater Britain" by people like Sir Charles Dilke who didn't really understand it) might have borne fruit as an "empire of many parliaments."

Everything herein about the astrophysics of Tau Ceti's planetary system is consistent with current knowledge, obtained through radial velocity planetary searches and presented in December 2012 in *Astronomy and Astrophysics*. It may be that future discoveries will knock all of this into a cocked hat—look at how the space probes have ruined the solar system!—but at this writing it's the best we've got.

The only liberty I have permitted myself concerns the fifth planet (Tau Ceti f, in the terminology of the exoplanet hunters, under which Earth would be "Sol d"; I've preferred to use the traditional system of Roman numerals for the planets, working outward, which seems to make better sense). I have assumed that the high end of the current estimate-range for its mass (6.6 ± 3.5 times that of Earth) is the correct figure, and that this total mass of 10.1 Earths is actually accounted for by a double-planet system. There is no positive evidence for this, but as far as I know it is not outside the bounds of possibility. All details of that double planet are, of course, products of authorial imagination; but, again, they involve no inherent impossibilities of which I am aware, and they incorporate the most current ideas regarding planetary habitability. Likewise my own are the names I've had the alternate-historical planet searchers assign to these planets... but they could do worse.

I have been equally faithful to the known facts concerning the Chi Eridani binary system, aside from the sub-stellar third companion, whose existence is merely suspected... and, of course, the Gharnakh presence there. Their habitat is an example of what has become known in our timeline as a "Bishop Ring" after Forrest Bishop, who originated the idea in 1997.

✧   ✧   ✧

For fictive purposes, I have postulated that this alternate timeline's technological development lagged about a generation behind our own history's up to the mid-twentieth century and then began to accelerate, allowing me to extrapolate as I chose from then to the late twenty-third century.

Would the world I have described use the same words as we ourselves do for such things as lasers (invented in our year 1959), astronomical units (a term first recorded in 1903), antimatter (coined in 1898), and so forth? Very likely not, but I have used them for the sake of clarity. I think I can justify the familiar science-fictional term "Gauss guns"; Carl Friedrich Gauss was born in 1777, and since this timeline does not begin to diverge radically from ours (especially outside Britain) until shortly after that, his life and works could well have been essentially the same.

The biographical sketch of the historical Robert Rogers in Chapter Two is factual up to and including his imprisonment by George Washington. Beyond that point, his story differs in this alternative timeline, as does so much else. As for Benedict Arnold, his betrayal of the revolution he had saved at Lake Champlain seems to have been largely motivated by revenge against personal enemies. If those enemies had taken a different road, as I have them doing, it is not unreasonable to suppose that he would have also done so in a kind of equal and opposite reaction.

General James Wilkinson's alternate-historical career path, as sketched in Chapter Eight, is consistent with his character as revealed in actual history. Quite simply, and without hyperbole, he was the most consummate scumbag ever to put on an American uniform. His career, which included two tenures as Commanding General of the United States Army, was marked by uninterrupted corruption, scandals, intrigues, cabals, and betrayal even of his own cohorts. He was a secret agent in the pay of Spain, to which he supplied advance notice of the Lewis and Clark expedition. He was involved in Aaron Burr's conspiracy to separate the West from the Union—and, of course, sold Burr out. Historian Robert Leckie characterized him as "a general who never won a battle or lost a court-martial." It is impossible to disagree with Theodore Roosevelt's judgment that "in all our history, there is no more despicable character." (Although personally I would award the title of most sheerly unpleasant character to the proto-totalitarian Thaddeus Stevens.) Fortunately, the United States was not involved in a major war for national survival on Wilkinson's watch, which is why he is largely forgotten today instead of living on in the annals of treason as he so richly deserves. By comparison, Vidkun Quisling was a paragon of nobility.